Sign Of The Times

I0192458

Cycle C Sermons for Advent, Christmas,
and Epiphany
Based on the Gospel Lessons

David Coffin

CSS Publishing Company, Inc.
Lima, Ohio

SIGN OF THE TIMES

FIRST EDITION
Copyright © 2024
by CSS Publishing Co., Inc.

Library of Congress Cataloging-in-Publication Data

Names: Coffin, David (Pastor), author.
Title: Sign of the times : cycle C sermons for Advent, Christmas, and
  epiphany based on the gospel lessons / David Coffin.
Description: First edition. | Lima, Ohio : CSS Publishing Company, Inc,
  [2024] | Includes bibliographical references.
Identifiers: LCCN 2024032314 | ISBN 9780788031137 | ISBN 9780788031144
  (ebook)
Subjects: LCSH: Advent sermons. | Christmas sermons. | Epiphany--Sermons. |
  Apocalyptic literature. | Preaching.
Classification: LCC BV4254.5 .C53 2024 | DDC 252/.61--dc23/eng/20240814
LC record available at https://lccn.loc.gov/2024032314

For more information about CSS Publishing Company resources, visit our website at www.csspub.com, email us at csr@csspub.com, or call (800) 241-4056.

e-book:
ISBN-13: 978-0-7880-3114-4
ISBN-10: 0-7880-3114-7

ISBN-13: 978-0-7880-3113-7
ISBN-10: 0-7880-3113-9

PRINTED IN USA

Contents

First Sunday In Advent
Luke 21:25-36

Sign Of The Times

Then he told them a parable: "Look at the fig tree and all the trees; as soon as they sprout leaves you can see for yourselves and know that summer is already near. So also, when you see these things taking place, you know that the kingdom of God is near. Luke 21: 29-31

Ever since I was a boy, these texts of the apocalyptic nature used to frighten me. We have a similar set of apocalyptic passages in Mark 13 and Matthew 24. Not to mention the entire Book of Revelation. Being raised in the 1960s, when there was much change, street violence and unpredictable weather patterns, I was vulnerable to latest populist evangelist book advertisements to get ready for the end of the world.

When I finally got to seminary in my second career, I was still fascinated with such interest in these "apocalyptic" or end of the world texts. I took classes on the books of Daniel and Revelation in my seminary years. From this I was met with the pleasant surprise that such books are intended to bring hope, confidence and affirm God's sovereign rule over the universe.

With that said, I committed myself to preaching and teaching how such apocalyptic texts could be practical for Christian living. I also preached about how they are not to be ignored and should be taken seriously. However, if there is good news in any bad news situation, it is the take away of such texts. I have a modern example below from past years of ministry.

"Stretch" was Wally's nickname because he was about six-feet and two inches tall; skinny with a dark beard and darker longer hair. He always wore dark brown work boots, blue jeans and grease-stained shirt. Stretch was the oldest child along with three girls in his family. He worked as a welder at a local metal fabrication shop after school while in senior high school. He hated school classes as he was better working with his hands. His school system did not have a vocational school program then. Stretch learned everything on the job. On the job training, the school of hard knocks and practice-makes-perfect were Stretch's learning slogans.

While in his senior year of high school, Stretch's father died. His mother had no real job skills, and had three girls to raise. The girls all did decently in school. Therefore, Stretch made the decision to quit school and work full time at the metal fabrication shop. His mom did babysitting and pet sitting for extra money. The three sisters were able to continue on through high school. One joined the Navy. The other got a job at the local greenhouse. The third sister did go to community college and got a job in a local accounting agency as the office manager.

Stretch read the signs of the times for his family. Their father was dead. He hated school, and he knew his sisters all liked school and wanted to get their high school diplomas. Stretch did get married finally and had a daughter who joined the armed forces. Stretch did not apologize for the decisions he made. In fact, he believes he is one of the better welders in the area. When people asked him what school he attended, he would tell them, "I went to the school of hard knocks."

Advent is a time when darkness has arrived as an old reality has come to an end, and a new one arrives. Luke's Gospel wants us to be able to read the "signs of the times" like knowing when the fig tree sprouts its leaves.

What signs of the times shall we consider today in our communities? This is an Advent question to grow spiritually in. In our times, we live after a pandemic period. Have we or will we ever get back to "normal?" Again, what sort of signs shall we be looking at for our present and future discipleship journey as Christians? Advent is the time to consider such questions.

One practical illustration I have experienced in post pandemic times is the nature of funerals. Though cremation existed before, I see more families taking this option. These families are very cost conscious, so they minimize the services of funeral homes. Thus, church sanctuaries are used as "visitation" locations for friends and family. Thus, a sign might be that congregational councils need to reassess building usage, custodian responsibilities, and questions about accessibility for physically challenged people. Now, more than ever, they are in the spotlight as guests with walkers and wheelchairs arrive more frequently.

In some communities, the funeral home provides bulletins plus contacts area newspaper and media outlets to provide the obituary notices. Is this now placed on the church office staff of any given congregation? If so, do job descriptions and costs need to be revisited? In a smaller church which is family centered, this might not seem to be a big deal — until out of state family members are involved in planning the funeral. Such family members may stay in area hotels and will leave after the funeral event. Without funeral homes as a liaison, what sorts of alternate plans are in place? If it occurs in winter time and certain states do not open graves in the snowy months, this also must be factored into any potential funeral.

When there is an illness or potential lapse of a loved one, the Advent word, "watch" becomes even more relevant. Entire families can possibly have their lives to be the equivalent of stars, earth, and moon distress and confusion of roaring chaos symbolized by the seas in scripture. In addition to these measures, one never knows when another form of influenza, or similar epidemic may occur in any given community. Are the communion kits with self-contained wafers and grape juice/wine now the new normal for people who have a lower immune system than younger, healthy people?

Finally, one of this of this week's word for Advent is the more urgent and real: "Watch!" That is keep your eyes open to the activities around you and observe certain patterns to see what the "signs of the times" are for us today? Do we know people who are at the edge of major change in their lives?

Another example might be, A 65-year-old woman has been working at an insurance agency for 29 years. She knows the clients and the business very well. Then her head insurance agent supervisor grows ill and dies. Perhaps a younger couple takes over the agency. They want to learn the business very quickly. Should this older office manager see the sign of the times? What will happen once the young couple settles down? The older office manager walked into work on Monday morning and was told, "You can go home now; we no longer need you here." The woman is age 65! She is to go onto Medicare in a couple months. However, her sister lives in the state capital where there are plenty of insurance jobs available. She has put her soul and heart into the small community for the past 29 years — is God calling her to leave and move to the capital city? This is an example of the signs of the times.

Advent is a season when the status quo we have grown familiar with just might leave us. We are in the dark and we sing "O Come, O Come Emanuel" in a very literal way! What does God have in store for us next? How do we grow as Christians during this "in between time?"

Advent was not intended to be "pre-Christmas." Rather it is a time of intense soul searching, reflection, and re-evaluating our life's journey as we are surrounded by darkness and look up at the stars and moon as our only guiding light. This is what the shepherds in the field did for many years.

In Luke's Gospel, Jesus' mission is, "to seek and save the lost" (Luke 19:10). Jesus does this through his teaching of parables that people of any religion can understand. All religions have a version of a "prodigal on." All religions have a version of "the good Samaritan." All religions know of a short, cheesy "Danny Devito" tax collector or slick money operator who is despised by most people in town — a Zacchaeus. Luke wanted to relate to people who do not always have a strong knowledge of the Old Testament [Hebrew Bible].

In each situation, Jesus shows how he is the Savior that points us to new life. Death is no longer the final word. Even on the cross, Jesus tells a repentant thief, "Today you will be with me in paradise" (Luke 23:43).

What are other signs of the times today? What modern fig trees might we observe during this Advent season? As we observe climate change, we may not be able to solve all of the ecological problems we see on the news weather channels. However, we can participate in community recycling efforts for trash and containers. We can be aware of using recycled paper products. And, we can take some time to clean any unnecessary clutter we might have in our homes, storage spaces or in the corner of a basement or attic.

Realizing that natural disasters have occurred since the days of the early Roman empire, we may always realize that the weather problem we see on the news in other locations may occur in our own backyards. Therefore, it might be a good act of stewardship to give money to faith-based disaster relief organizations which often arrive at places of weather destruction sooner than government agencies who often have to deal with much, complex red tape before taking action.

As the health care industry and insurance trends tend to be a perpetual roller coaster, what sort of health practices might we explore during Advent. Many people do make New Year's resolutions related to losing weight, only to be broken before month's end. However, smaller, incremental, realistic measures might be considered. Examples might include being purposeful in some communities where drinking water can no longer be taken for granted. Any given city can become a "Flint, Michigan" at any given time due to either poor administrative decision making or shortages of natural water supplies.

What will the future of small churches look like after some key church members are no longer in a position to support the congregations? These are "Advent questions." Such question can be asked at any time of a given year. For example, such questions one asks while in the "waiting room of a medical office or auto repair shop." The word here is to, "watch" for the sign of the times.

The good news is that God is not finished with us here in our churches, regardless of how dark or bright the days are ahead. We can go to sleep at night with the confidence that through the death and resurrection of Jesus the Christ, there is always new life.

As a closing thought is a high school wrestling coach that was at an east coast high school coaching the sport of wrestling. Due to school financial cut backs, the wrestling program had to be downsized and later discontinued because basketball was the most popular winter sport in that school system. The coach saw neighboring school systems doing the same thing in terms of putting more money into their basketball programs. The coach went online and found out that in a remote western state, which is almost half way across the country they need wrestling coaches really badly! So, does he persist in his city life in along east coast while scrimping for a substitute teacher job — or does he move himself and family out to western Iowa where wrestling is doing just great? What is the sign of the times? As churches, we also need to be watching for the sign of the times in those areas of our lives that we value. This is where God meets us and molds our faith in Advent.

Amen.

Works Cited

- John T. Carroll, *The New Testament Library: Luke,* Westminster John Knox Press, 2012.

- Chen, Diane G., *New Covenant Commentary Series: Luke,* Eugen, OR: Cascade Books, 2017.

Second Sunday of Advent
Luke 3:1-6

Prepare

...Prepare the way of the Lord, make his paths straight. Luke 3:4

Where did you get your first life experiences regarding church? One of the modern discussions regarded to how to deal with the uncertain future of the church, is to share our own stories or life narratives about what is good about the church. I am one who has enjoyed retreats put on by churches where people are away from the stress of their work and other concerns, usually at a retreat center of some resort away from the mainstream traffic of everyday life stresses. Believe it or not, for me it was summer church camp that brought me the fondest memories.

I believe that church camp experiences often shape and prepare who we are as people of faith. They remain with us as we prepare for life. One of my favorite stories was doing "KP" duty in the camp kitchen. It was the most dreaded job in the camp. It entailed scrubbing out huge pots, pans, and baking pans that were as big as I was a kid. It meant sweeping the dining mess from the floors and if necessary, peeling potatoes for the next meal. In return, the workers got some extra food from the leftovers.

I gladly did my time in KP duty. When the time came for our "tribe" (they did the Indian tribe thing then as a way to name dormitories), to go swimming, the counselor hesitantly asked for volunteers to work KP. I raised my hand up frantically! Soon, I became a pretty popular kid who "liked doing KP" duty all the time.

But my dirty little secret was that I was afraid of water and swimming in the water. I learned about cooking at an early age in the church camp cafeteria. Fast forward to my years in college. I met my biological dad whom my mom divorced when I was three-years-old. He told me that in the US Navy he was afraid of water, so he volunteered for KP duty on the ship. Soon, he became a very popular man on board the ship. He became the "chef's mate" – first class even!

On a hot, sticky day, when everybody wanted to jump overboard ship to swim, my biological dad gladly went to the kitchen to work KP. All the officers and crew were *pleased as punch to have him on board.* To think that my camp story and my dad's Navy story "connected," did much to prepare me in life. Today's Advent theme is *"Prepare."*

Luke 3 has the infancy and ministry narrative of John Baptist to help us *"prepare"* in Advent. Today's sermon will have two points: 1) The *Man* Who Prepares 2) The *Message* That Prepares.

The two thoughts that all scholars want readers to know about this text is first that God took the initiative to come down to humans! This is important because royalty always had their subjects come to them — even if it was an annual pilgrimage. Luke's Gospel goes into much detail to document who was the ruling Caesar at that time, being Tiberius Caesar; who was the Tetrarch of that day, being Herod, as well as the ruling priesthood Annas and Caiaphas. Despite any problems later historians have with Luke's dating, he is using the technology he has available to him at that time. This is not unlike a person using a rotary telephone to communicate with friends and neighbors, it does not diminish the value of the exchange of ideas or conversation when a later time cell phones and androids are used for the same purposes.

Second, many religions have been about humans seeking their "god" or "true meaning of life." In Luke, God finds us. We do not find God. This is the doctrine of "grace." Today's lesson wants us to see who God chooses to prepare us for the great coming of the Messiah.

> John the Baptist was Jesus' cousin. He was of a Jewish family. This is important to indicate that Jesus and his family were "common working folks" for their times.
>
> John the Baptist was "rough around the edges" in his manners and appearance. This was not the kid who was groomed to be a lawyer, diplomat, doctor, or teacher. He was the man or woman who would tell you, "I have learned life's lessons in the 'school of hard knocks.'"
>
> Modern examples include that John the Baptist was the "pit crew" who was behind the scenes of a race car driver's fame. John the Baptist was the "stage hands and lighting people" before the big play or theatre presentation." John the Baptist was the worker in the back room who got the phone when the office staff was gone to lunch. He had a rough speaking demeanor. He was not a big talker. When

he did say things, they were not "polished or well thought-out." This man called the king's woman a "harlot." He spoke his mind — even if was in trouble. God used such people to keep us on our toes and remind us that anything is possible with God. So be prepared.

Back in seminary church history class, I learned that Martin Luther's father Hans was a miner and worked another job as a tailor so his boy Martin could go to law school. When his boy Martin said he made a promise to Saint Anne to become a monk, the older Hans was not too thrilled! He was gruff and angry! He was hoping to get his family out of the working class by having Martin go to law school. Martin had the brains to do this! Why waste a life on the church? But Luther became more than a monk and of course initiated the Protestant Reformation.

Still Hans Luther was pretty rough and unforgiving as old stubborn Germans go. But God worked through the family and name of this old stubborn German. This might be an example of a John the Baptist who unknowingly prepared his son to change Europe and the world.

The second point of my sermon is the *message* that prepares. The people of Israel were awaiting another voice from God since the days of Ezra and Malachi. For them, God was "silent" for 400 years in the intertestamental period. This has come into some scholarly debate, as many scholars date the Book of Daniel during the intertestamental time period.

With that said, John the Baptist was preaching a word of "repentance." For John, this meant actually living out what we believe to be right. For John, this meant bearing the fruits of the faith. Later on in the text, John indicated what he meant by fruits: Whoever has two coats, share with somebody who has none. Tax collectors are to simply be honest and not collect any more taxes than they should. Soldiers and people in power are not abuse their power or try to extort people for money (Luke 3:10-14).

John's idea of "fruits" was to lead a quality of life that was in agreement with the Ten Commandments and doing God's will, as we know it to be in the teachings from scripture.

A good test here might be if we knew that we would die in three months, how would we conduct our Christian life any differently?

From John the Baptist's point of view, if we were living out a consistent life of discipleship, we would not change hardly anything in how we live.

As this relates to Advent and Christmas — God can come into our lives at any time and do something unexpected! John the Baptist said we needed to prepare ourselves by simply living out the best Christian life we know how to live.

As a pastor living in a modern high-tech era after the pandemic, I observe many congregations that have taken to having a social media platform so people can watch their worship services on one of the many YouTube, Facebook, or other media platforms. If smaller congregations who are on tight budgets invest in such electronic equipment, how much longer would costs for upgrading such equipment reach unreasonable prices for smaller churches?

It is like a state that promises to fund a new school building as a means of progress. The school is usually asked to provide a smaller portion of matching funds. So far so good for such fiscally challenged schools with declining students' enrollment and often less tax base. The unstated expectations are usually the school then has to pay for upgrades of cooling, heating, safety, and other modern technical convenience. Are they prepared to meet such often unforeseen costs for upkeep?

It occurs to me, that as we read John the Baptist's word today, the prophet suggested that we practice our faith in a very purposeful manner — everyday. I observe that many of us do exactly that in this season. We do this with our giving to others in need, being generous with our resources, and working within our communities to serve others in need.

I recently read a book by Rick Herrick, titled, *"Moving Beyond Belief: A New Focus for the Christian Faith,"* (Eugene, OR: Wipf and Stock, 2022). One of Herrick's recurring themes was that the modern Christian church religion needs to move beyond defining our beliefs as personal salvation in order to secure a place in the afterlife. Jesus dedicated his life to bringing in the kingdom of God into the world right now as we currently live on this planet. Furthermore, a religion that simply confesses beliefs during worship but does not translate into actually works against the vision of the kingdom of God. It easily translates into self-righteous efforts to acquire more goods and attempts to care for only those immediately in our world, without regard for concerns of global hunger, poverty, and climate change.

History has shown that without actually practicing what Jesus taught, it is easy to use the church as an entrance ramp for power-brokers to climb up into the political hierarchy. At this writing, Rick Herrick is concerned that the state religion of Russia is being used to bless any aggressive military action against neighbors [Ukraine]. This appears to be similar to the ancient Roman empire using their religious beliefs to justify emperor worship.

On this Advent Sunday, Luke proclaimed that God was keeping his promises by arriving in the form of a Messiah that follows the Isaiah tradition from what scholars call the "book of comfort" beginning in Isaiah 40. This is the suffering servant model. This is how God chooses to enter our world after 400 years of silence from the Old Testament [Hebrew Bible].

John the Baptist simply wants us to prepare by doing the daily Christian discipleship ministries that our Lord demonstrated for us before he died on the cross for our sins and rose from the grave three days later. We are now called to prepare to be fruitful as a response to this salvation.

Today, to prepare is not "rocket science." We have this prophet, who though is a little rough around the edges tells us to do what we know to be the right things to do. Our task as a church is to continue to teach and sing about this ministry in our worship and Christian education ministries here at our church.

Another tool of the faith is one I share in my catechism classes; I use an acronym I once learned in Sunday school as a child — Advent is HOPE = How One Prepares Every day .

As a conclusion, in one of the episodes of "The Simpson's," Reverend Lovejoy was in a faith crisis as he saw Homer's wife Marge Simpson as able or more able than he — to do crisis counseling. The depressed Reverend Lovejoy went to play with his electric trains as his hobby. Toward the end of the episode, the Simpson's Christian neighbor, Ned Flanders was being chased by bullies to the local zoo. Ned Flanders was trapped in a wild baboon den in the zoo. Reverend Lovejoy was quick enough to jump onto the zoo's train ride and grab Ned Flanders out of the baboon den. Reverend Lovejoy was prepared, not by being inspired, but simply by keeping up on his train hobby — even when he was down and out. Today, God works in our midst everyday as we live out the faithful lives of discipleship.

Amen.

Works Cited

- Chen, Diane G., *New Covenant Commentary Series: Luke,* Eugen, OR: Cascade Books, 2017.

- Herrick, Rick, *Moving Beyond Belief: A New Focus for the Christian Faith,* Eugen, OR: Wipf and Stock, 2022.

Third Sunday of Advent
Luke 3:7-18

Advent Story

About a month or so before he died, my theology professor Dr. Walt Bouman of Trinity Lutheran Seminary told me that without the theology of the cross and resurrection, George Patton is right, [language cleaned-up] "No person ever won a war by dying for his country. He won it by making the other poor dumb person die for their country." However, this is not the final word of our gospel.

In the 1970 movie, *"Patton,"* George C. Scott played the very opinionated and, yes, skillful General Patton. After the US Troops got defeated in their first battle in North Africa in the year 1942, General Omar Bradley wanted "the best tank commander we've got." General Patton was called in. Patton was a battlefield genius. He quickly established discipline among his troops. He commanded with an "iron fist." He respected his enemies so much that he read German General Rommel's books. The Germans in Berlin who studied him noted that he was a romantic, read the Bible daily, swore like a stable boy, and believed in reincarnation. He loved the limelight, so he always advanced his troops further than where he was ordered. He was always in a race to the next battle.

General Patton was also controversial. He slapped a [shell-shocked] soldier's helmet. He routinely insulted the Russian and British Allies. He had a short temper. Patton's ego created so much trouble among the allies that General Eisenhower had to tell him to shut up and stay out of trouble. Today, George Patton might be like John the Baptist whose opening words to the crowds were, "You brood of vipers! Who warned you to flee from the wrath to come?" He is no diplomat and I am not sure you would want this man reading bedtime stories to the children.

We may not like a Patton or John the Baptist. With that said — What story is your Christian life telling today? This is the challenge of our text.

Traditionally, John the Baptist was the prophet who was predicted in both Isaiah 40 and Malachi 3. For 400 years, the people cried for a prophet and yearned to hear more words from God. This is what the Christian Church calls the "intertestament period."

When they finally got their prophet, he was a strong man of God, but about as "unrefined and ill-mannered" as General George Patton. Thus, we have the opening sentence, "You brood of vipers!"

John was an independent prophet who was neither under the secular or religious credential authorization of his time. Today, in politics, he would be running as an "independent candidate." John spoke his mind. He preached "repentance." The Greek word is *mentanoia*. John was the GPS direction finder in one's car that has a loud and maybe rough voice.

Luke recorded that John's baptism and ministry were the beginning of Jesus' ministry. John was mad at the people who were looking for a "minimal way" to get right with God. John opposed the "get out of hell free card," salvation. John would have been critical of people who think "just being a member is not good enough if one does not walk their talk." John was what Martin Luther would call the voice of the "law....you are trying to pull a fast one on God by saying if you belong to the family of Abraham, that is good enough....God can make stones in a nation."

You need a savior! God can turn stones into humans who call themselves children of Abraham.

The "irony" of the "stone" metaphor is later in the gospel, the stone that the builders rejected in Luke 20:17 has become the cornerstone of the foundation of the kingdom. This stone would be the Messiah who was rejected by the masses, crucified on the cross and rose from the grave three days later. He was and is Jesus the Christ.

John would pay a price for his very rough and loud ministry later, when King Herod would arrest him. To call people a brood of vipers suggested they eat or consume their young or upcoming generations as vipers tend to do. It suggests that they only care about getting their own slice of the modern economic pie at the expense of more vulnerable upcoming generations. This is a harsh critique for anybody who holds a leadership or modern shepherding office. Are we willing to take the risk and exclaim, "What is the matter does the truth hurt?" I am not sure many people in our congregation have the calling to be this candid or use such harsh language.

If we do not want the blunt, rough message style of a John the Baptist, how does God get our attention? What story are each of us here our community telling — with our Christian lives and living? This is the Advent challenge…what story do people actually see in us if they were to look at us every day?

One of the discussions I am hearing in a denomination sponsored course on "engaging God's future," is how a congregation can grow beyond survival mode, where most of the council meetings are about the building, budget, and volunteers into a thriving people of the kingdom who are making a difference for God where they live? What is the narrative we wish to share with our congregation about proclaiming the good news in both word and action? Are we simply a stone that rests on the ground and declares we are Abraham's children? What would be a good two-minute elevator speech to share about our congregation as we seek to thrive rather than survive?

One example might be, "We are a very small congregation. However, we host both a recycling drive and food pantry ministry to people in the community who are on fixed incomes. If an emergency comes up, simply call the church and somebody will get back to you as to when they can meet to provide a small bag of groceries.

Another narrative might be that we are the church near a college who offers to host students for meals and a place to call a "home away from home" when they are weary of campus dormitory life and cafeteria food.

In one church, there was a small church ministry that offered confirmation instruction to students who are academically challenged or as some schools use to call them, "special needs" students who rode on a different bus than the rest of the students.

While such ministry narratives may not translate into church growth in numbers or membership, they are examples of bringing in the kingdom of God. They are living out the faith of Abraham which John is calling out religious leaders to consider.

These are examples of how any size congregation and Christian in any congregation can be a nurturing presence which meets people in awkward situations in life. It is to such an audience that John in Luke, as well as Jesus in Luke, was often addressing as an example of the kingdom of God.

What John the Baptist was calling for people of faith to do was not to quit our jobs and go into full time ministry or professional church service but to practice our Christian faith where we are now. Luke's Gospel provides examples from John the Baptist that might include in his vision for the kingdom. For example, to those who have abundance, are we sharing with those in need? Luke 10 would later show the good Samaritan who helped a man who was robbed on the road.

Tax collectors can remain tax collectors — but do not cheat people. Treat them fairly. Luke 19 would show us this with Zacchaeus who invited Jesus into his home and changed his ways.

The soldiers do not use their power to take advantage of people under Rome's rule. The best example of this is that centurion in Luke 7:6-9, "Lord do you trouble yourself, for I am not worthy to have you come under my roof; therefore, I did not presume to come to you. But only speak the word, and let my servant be healed. For I also am a man set under authority, with soldiers under me; and I say to one, 'Go,' and he goes, and to another, 'Come,' and he comes, and to my slave, 'Do this,' and the slave does it. When Jesus heard this, he was amazed at him, and turning to the crowd following him, he said, "I tell you, I have not found such great faith even in Israel." This soldier trusts Jesus to heal his servant.

As Martin Luther might put it, the problem or "law" is that we often take shortcuts in life. We try to find the easy way out of solving difficult problems, then wake up one day and wonder what sort of mess we have on our hands now.

These past years have repeatedly shown more mass shootings in various settings and in assorted cities or suburban neighborhoods. May we suggest that God is in the midst of this? Advent is the season to remind us of another Advent theme to always be prepared for anything to occur in our lives. This is why we need to always let our loved ones know that we "care" for them (even if they annoy us sometimes). We need to treat every day as if it is a gift from God. Every day, I tell my wife that I love her, even when we are in a hurry or rushed to get to another destination.

In Advent, this is where the text is pushing us toward spiritual growth. John the Baptist is not telling anybody to quit a job and join a monastery or go to divinity school — but simply be the presence of Jesus wherever we work, live, or study. One does not have to be a big church to do this! One does not need the latest high-tech equipment to do this. No, it is a matter of spiritual tools of: prayer, the Bible, being in fellowship, and caring for others.

A closing thought : a man recently got out of the local jail for driving under the influence. He was given a list of churches where there were Alcoholics Anonymous meetings occurring. He felt down and out and defeated. He went to an area church to see cars parked all around the lot. Slowly, he opened the back door and walked into a huge fellowship hall with people all sitting at the tables eating a full meal with meat, potatoes, vegetables, salads, and desserts. There was plenty of coffee there. He felt awkward but he asked one of the people if the pastor was there. He thought this was where the AA meeting was held. The pastor and a church elder came to the man and told him the AA meeting is not meeting here that week, but down the road due to their church's Christmas meal. However, this man was more than invited and to sit down and have a bite to eat with the church people, fellowship, and sing Christmas hymns. The tired man smelled the food and accepted the invitation to enjoy the Christmas meal with this church. Eventually he found his way to a different Alcoholics Anonymous meeting location. This meal made him want to return to worship at this church on Sunday and bring a family member with him. From that time on, he attended the church and always wanted to help with the coffee hour following worship. This might be an example of a person who came out of a very harsh environment of the state corrections system and walked into a meal of Advent and Christmas season hope. Hope is what this season of Advent is all about. Are there people we know who are weary from rough experiences in life who can use a simple church dinner? This is where God is found on this Advent Sunday. A meal can be a speak in a louder voice than harsh words of criticism.

Amen.

Works Cited

- "Patton." AMC. *DirecTV*. n.d.

- Carroll, John. *The New Testament Library: Luke*. Louisville, KY: Westminster John Knox Press, 2012.

- Vinson, Richard. *Smyth & Hewlys Bible Commentary: Luke*. Macon, GA: Smyth & Hewlys, 2008.

Fourth Sunday of Advent
Luke 1:39-55

Magnify The Lord

And Mary said, "My soul magnifies the Lord. Luke 1:45

In the 1965 movie, *"Sound of Music,"* Marie who was a governess married Captain Georg von Trapp, only to have their world brought down around them by the 1938 in Austria, where Nazi Germany takes control of the country. The Nazis demanded that Captain von Trapp assume a position in the German Navy. In a scene where the family was singing a farewell song, they sang the song and invited the audience to sing the words of "Edelweiss," — bless my homeland forever.

In the Luke 1, this text is often called a hymn. Like the movie *"Sound of Music,"* the characters broke out in a song! This particular text is often called the *"Magnificat."* This means it "magnifies" or "enlarges" a particular area in one's life.

In the movie *"Sound of Music,"* the reality was that nation of Austria was about to go through some very dark, horrible years as it was being annexed by the German Nazis. It was in fact, not the "old country" that people had cherished. But the von Trapp family chose to sing the song of "Edelweiss…bless my homeland forever". They were "magnifying" the homeland of Austria!

In Luke's Gospel, the days of Roman occupation were the reality. Rome was an empire who used brutal tactics to keep people in line. They taxed the nations they ruled with a heavy hand! The government was corrupt.

Saint Luke's Gospel goes into much detail to "document" who was in charge at this time, so that nobody can later deny their corruption or plead plausible deniability. Specific dates and details of time that may not match modern historical research need not be an issue. Luke works with the technology has. We would not compare a person who communicated through a party line rotary telephone with the person who used hand-held Android devices. The content of the conversations remain valid as does the reality of the existence of these people as well as their presence in certain events. However, Mary chose to magnify what God was doing right at that time in her life.

The text is generally seen as a time when Mary wisely sought the advice and counsel of an elderly woman named Elizabeth. This supported the idea that older people have wisdom to offer younger people and it is worth any travel time to obtain such wisdom.

The text is also of the Proverbs 31 tradition of a seasoned woman and Proverbs 1 tradition of wisdom being most powerful of all forces that transcends time. "The fear of the Lord is beginning of all knowledge; fools despise wisdom and instruction" (Proverbs 1:7).

Another Old Testament [Hebrew Bible] tradition of 1 Samuel is when Hannah, a humble woman was about to bear Israel's great prophet, Samuel. God's meeting with the humble woman with little means within a patriarchal society is more of the good news we read throughout Luke's Gospel. We read about a sinful woman anointing and kissing Jesus' feet with an alabaster jar of oil. As a response to Jesus' acceptance and love for her at the home of a critical Pharisee, Jesus used this as a teaching moment to speak of debts and forgiveness (Luke 7:36-50). Later in Luke 9, Jesus would heal a woman suffering from a hemorrhage who touched him in a crowd, along with a leader's daughter who was in stages of death (Luke 8:40-55).

It is the first time that Jesus, before he was even born was called, "Lord" or the Greek word is *Kyrios*. Another Greek word that describes where God was working in power or the Greek word is *dunatos* from *dunamis*, meaning power — where we get "dynamite" through a poor, humble woman with lowly status in the community. It is amidst an obscure, non-royal celebrity that the mighty God of creation and Israel is doing a powerful act of coming as Lord to the earth.

This is why Mary and Elizabeth were singing! Rome thought it was in control, but God was doing something even more powerful in the coming birth. In the tradition of Genesis 18:14, when Sarah who was older in age was told she would have a child, she was reminded that nothing is too difficult or wonderful for God. This provides hope to anybody today who feels they are in a hopeless situation with their health, finances, job, family, or any other area of their life. If God can provide Sarah a child, Advent's hope reminds us that God can do anything. This is good news of the text.

Some other good news of this text is that for those of us who lack: prestige and wealth, or are of the privileged in our society — God still works through us. It will be the lower profile, insignificant people of the community whom God reveals God's mighty acts such as later to the shepherds in Luke 2:8-19.

A modern example might be what if somebody is not going to have too great of a Christmas holiday? Suppose rather than identifying with the familiar Christmas New Testament texts, a person felt more like the book of Ecclesiastes?

In one of the of the upcoming Hebrew Bible [Old Testament] texts in Pentecost 8 and Ecclesiastes 1:12-14 we may capture some of these feelings during this Advent season before Christmas, "I, the teacher when king over Israel in Jerusalem, applied my mind to seek and to search out by wisdom all that is done under the heavens; it is unhappy business that God has given to human beings to be busy with. I saw all the deeds that are done under the sun; and see all is vanity and chasing after the wind. What is crooked cannot be made straight" (Ecclesiastes 1:12-15).

An example of the futility and unfairness in life that the Book of Ecclesiastes so observes, can occur — even during the holidays. Imagine a medical care facility where the upper management arranges it so only the supervisors, key management personnel, and friends of the management staff have arranged the schedule so they are the only people who get the week off between Christmas and New Year. Furthermore, they are able to get a couple of three-day weekends out this arrangement.

Meanwhile, the regular workers on the floor, the caregivers and frontline office staff must come to work throughout the week between Christmas and New Year. The book of Ecclesiastes would suggest that life is not fair. Manipulative people often get rewarded at the expense of good, hard-working people who toil under the sun. This is reality. The fear of God is still a good thing (Ecclesiastes 12:13).

Luke's lesson today would remind these workers that God is mysteriously with those workers who remain on the job during the Christmas week. God is indeed capable to "[bring] down the powerful from their thrones, and lift up the lowly" (Luke 1:52). From a distant point of view, one never knows when management on all levels in any organization can lose their positions due to corporate changes or shakeups. In the immediate future, in this case the patients appreciated the labor of the medical facility workers, and brought assorted gifts in wrapping paper for those who remained on the job. God has spoken to such people through the gifts of appreciation provided by the patients and their families. This might be both a way of responding to the unfairness in life that Ecclesiastes reported, as well as pointing to the real spirit of the season, which is providing hope, joy, and comfort in difficult times.

Finally, God is present in those who do work the holiday and weekend hours when everybody else is gone. As with Mary in her song, Advent reminds them that anything can happen with the God of scripture!

One of the other issues of Luke's Gospel, which will always come up is that of money and wealth. Luke did not oppose money and wealth — per se. He opposed its abuse.

Luke believed that there would be a reversal of fortunes, or the "shoe would be on the other foot one day." Mary would be honored throughout time in the church. Even people in the Islamic faiths respect her. This was to be contrasted to the "rich fool" in Luke 12. This man got a huge bumper crop. He decided he would hoard his possessions and build a bigger barn. The Lord says, "You fool, this very night your life will be demanded of you. And the things you prepared, whose will they be?" (Luke 12:20).

This text is so powerful that in seminary we were taught that in some countries where there is a dictator who controls everybody and everything, this Luke song of the "Magnificat" is forbidden reading. Why? Because it says, "He has brought down the powerful from their thrones, and lifted up the lowly; he has filled the hungry with good things, and sent the rich away empty. He has helped his servant Israel; in remembrance of his mercy, according the promise he made to our ancestors, to Abraham and his to his descendants forever" (Luke 1:52-55). This means that God is capable of reversals. God keeps his promises. Other examples include when a salesperson is promoted to sales manager while the sales manager is demoted back to regular salesperson.

The student may one day become the teacher or employee of the one who uses power-bully tactics to teaches them now. Finally, everybody will have an aging body which may no longer be able to function in as in times past. The person who is the caregiver, my one day become the care receiver.

Luke uses every day, regular people to make points of where God's power is active.

Today, God is active amidst two poor women who are about to give birth to children and they are in some mountain home sharing stories. Rome is still the brutal empire it always has been. The chances that that both boys of these women will be in conflict with Rome. One will die on the cross for the sins of humanity, but he would rise from the grave. Those who confess him as Savior and Lord would indeed have life. Right then the women called him "Lord." One day his lordship would be for the whole world. This is why these women were singing. Just like in the *Sound of Music* movie, the Nazi Third Reich would eventually fall. But an obscure von Trapp family would have their story told on millions of movie and TV screens.

As I was writing this sermon, there had been many shootings in schools during these past few years. I am struck by how school teachers and staff these days are fully aware that they not only instruct children and perform their respective job description, but may be called upon to protect young students in any natural disaster or act of school violence. It is a reminder that when any school system supports the costs of their building and programs, they are also paying for teachers and staff who often put their lives on the line for the lives of young children in schools. They are not just paying workers who put in their time, but people who genuinely care and love the students they teach. Therefore, I am one who believes we need to magnify and celebrate anybody who works in our community schools in any position from custodian up through administrators. I have no problem singing their songs or uplifting their local school colors. What song has moved you to want to magnify a certain group of people? This is the story I would prefer to see "magnified" on this day.

To close, I wish to share a song that both magnifies my better senses and drives me a bit stir crazy. On one hand, I really enjoy seeing special reports showing young children in the hospital either recovering from surgery or undergoing some level of cancer treatment, who can still sing "Jingle Bells." It lifts my heart up to see such joy, which should be magnified. On the other hand, before I became a pastor, I used to drive to work during bad weather while listening to the radio in the morning. About this time of year, they would play the barking dogs who barked to the tune of "Jingle Bells." This irritated me to the point where I wanted to hurry up to get to work or simply turn off the radio. To this very day, the barking dogs version of the song "Jingle Bells" annoys me, but it also prompts me to get on with my day.

Maybe this is another mysterious way God uses songs and music to magnify God's presence.

Amen.

Works Cited

- Carroll, John. *The New Testament Library: Luke.* Louisville, KY: Westminster John Knox Press, 2012.
- Hallmark Channel. *DirecTV.* December 2022.

The Nativity Of Our Lord
Luke 2:1-20

God Enters Into Our World

And she gave birth to her firstborn son and wrapped him in bands of cloth, and laid him in a manger, because there was no place for them in the inn. Luke 2:7

This year I would like to suggest that the first Christmas for the family of Jesus may not have been like a Hallmark movie or Christmas card. Let me illustrate: Every year when the Department of Motor Vehicles sends me an envelope asking me if I wish to renew my license plate tags through the mail or go to the local DMV at the county seat, I immediately fill out the form and send in the check! Why? I dread going to the Department of Motor Vehicle office in any town. I have been in the offices in: Detroit, Michigan, Columbus, and Toledo, Ohio. Even our county seat here in Iowa was not as long for me, but the guy there has given me a hard time — so I try to avoid these places, even here in Iowa. For me, the DMV are places of perpetual disorganization, chaos, and usually the "right hand does not know what the left hand is doing."

In some states, one gets one of those numbers off the spool. Then they must wait until their number is called. There are usually three or four windows or lines. One is for cars, one is for trailers, one is for motorcycles, and one is for other vehicles. Which window we wait at is always a mystery for me. It is usually crowded. The chairs are uncomfortable. Nowadays, people are talking on cell phones. Sometimes the people waiting there have poor hygiene, so they smell badly, have tobacco on their breath, or the baby's diaper needs to be changed.

The workers behind the counters are yelling out numbers. And if more congestion is to occur, it is because one of the computers broke down, the camera for pictures is broke or the power flicks on and off — so every machine needs to reboot and if a person was in line, then, they must re-do their form. By the time I get out of one of these places, my nerves are on edge. I have a stress headache and need a Tylenol® And I feel as if my whole day was "gutted or wasted."

On Christmas Eve, Hallmark and other commercial interests portray a: tranquil, peaceful scene with a star shining above. Angels are in the sky singing and there are shepherds as well as wise men guarding the baby Jesus. This is the image of the Hallmark and commercial holiday folks. The stories usually end up with all the loose ends tied up and the characters live happily forever and ever. The handsome couple finds one another. The children's get their dream holiday, and villains disappear from the scenes.

It is not necessarily the image one gets from biblical texts such as Luke 2. In fact, the setting is closer to a visit at the local DMV when it is crowded and people need to get their licenses renewed before midnight! Luke's Gospel seeks to be very historically accurate in locating the birth of Jesus into real world history! The whole trip to Bethlehem for the family of Joseph is another example of Roman imperial exploitation of the masses who had no vote in the matter.

The rulers who were in office took a census for purposes of taxes. It is not contested by any scholars — Rome had no problem wasting people's time, energy, and personal resources and allowing them to get caught up in bureaucratic red tape! And yes, the right hand in the government does not know what the left hand is doing, so many people get left out to wait — or have their lives "put on hold for an indefinite period of time."

Thus, we have the setting in Luke 2. The inn was not so much of a Holiday Inn sort of place where the desk clerk says, "there are no rooms" — so the family can go stay in the barn *or* the garage. Nope, it is more like a community building the refugee families all crowd into after a hurricane or an earthquake that have displaced people from their homes and FEMA has not arrived yet. So, the people are staying in quick-to-assemble cots.

In those days, they brought all their animals inside with them. Thieves and wandering livestock would result in total loss. People kept an eye on all their animals, chickens, cows, and all.

It is in this type of crowded chaos is where we have the birth of the Lord or God in the flesh, named God entered our world in one of the worst possible scenarios of the times so God can experience the realities of humankind. He came into the most disorganized, chaotic circumstances possible for those days.

In the 1980 Movie, *Brubaker,* starring Robert Redford, Henry Brubaker entered a corrupt southern prison farm as a prisoner in the prison's truck. As a prisoner, he witnessed much stealing, illegal activities, and violence. After breaking up a fight and being taken into the warden's office, Brubaker announced that he, Henry Brubaker, was the new prison warden who has just been appointed by the governor's office. God enters our world in similar circumstances.

When God came into the world, the shepherds were the first group of people to get the news (Luke 2:8). The shepherds of that time were non-skilled peasants who were sent out into the fields at night where danger lurks with outlaws and wild animals. They were seen as the "expendable" labor force in which there were plenty of replacements. Their job description did not even appear on the radar screen of the Google or US News' "Top Ten Careers" of their time. Once they died, there was a line around the employment office awaiting their jobs.

In the Hebrew Bible, we have two examples of God working through people of little or no social status. The first is Hannah in 1 Samuel 1-2. Here was a humble woman of faith who needed to bear a child in order to have offspring. In that culture and time, the offspring were responsible for caring and supporting older family members. It was their version of a "social security" plan to maintain minimal subsistence in their elderly years. Hannah was barren, but prayed to God. Her prayer is ten verses long in 1 Samuel 2:1-10. With her husband Elkanah, she did bear a son and named him Samuel. She was true to her word and promises to God and gave him over to the temple as a Nazarite (1 Samuel 1:21). Hannah would later conceive three other sons and two daughters. God did bless Hannah for her faithfulness.

Samuel was raised in the temple by Eli right next to Eli's two sons Hophni and Phinehas, who were often abusive of the power and privileges offered to them as the priest's sons. Though his sons disgraced Eli, God still was capable of reversals and miracles. The boy whom Hannah dedicated to the temple, would later become one of God's great prophets who would also have an eye for the least likely candidates for positions of power and blessing, such as the shepherd boy.

In 1 Samuel 16, God sent the prophet Samuel to anoint one of Jesse's sons as king. Jesse brought out all his big, strapping warrior sons to be inspected by Samuel. God did not want any of these sons. Then Jesse, mentioned the shepherd boy as an "after thought," as though "he should not to be considered for any office. He did not have the skill set or personality type to be a king. However, this shepherd boy was exactly who Samuel wanted. He would be King David.

Today, God reveals himself to people whom we think are the least likely candidates as messengers of God. They might be seasonal help at big box stores, or unemployed artists with tattoos on their body trying to make money through panhandling or singing on an old guitar with a donation can next to them.

Finally, Luke 2 reminds us that Mary treasured all these words of the shepherds, angels, and birth events in her heart. The shepherds went to spread the word. For Luke, God is still working in the history of salvation here in our community through events such as the humble birth, and words of the lowly shepherds. If one wishes to see where God is bringing in new life, this text suggests it is not in a state-of-the-art modern medical facility which has the latest technology at its disposal. Rather it may be in a remote distant rural medical clinic, inner city emergency room or possibly in the back of an EMS vehicle enroute to the closest medical facility. The miracle of Christmas continues to be that God can do great acts in the least likely places through people whom are not usually associated with the technology, financial or scientific leaders of the day. This is who the shepherds were in Luke's Gospel.

This challenges each of us here in our church to be people who share the good news of birth of a new Messiah who points us to new life regardless of what kind of difficult circumstances we are experiencing in finances, family problems, addictions, community concerns, or worries about extended family in other regions of the country. One observation to make is quite often twelve-step recovery support groups who often meet in church buildings still meet and support one another even and especially on any given holiday. The twelve-step support group members realize they need the help of their higher power — especially when the rest of the local gatherings are gathering to consume liquor and celebrate the holidays in whatever way they interpret them as reason. In fact, some twelve-step groups have a higher attendance in lieu of family at home who view holidays as a time to disrespect other people's boundaries and sensitivities. This might be one of the most important urgent and important ministries of any given church who hosts such twelve-step meeting groups. It is another place of entry for God into the world on this Nativity of our Lord's Day of the year.

People know Christ through us. This baby would grow up. He would die for the sins of humanity. He would rise from the grave three days later. In the birth account of Luke 2, we see such vulnerability and humility is most powerful and wise occurring to empower, equip, and bring hope to people here in our state. In Luke's Gospel, Jesus' mission is to seek and to save the lost (Luke 19:10). It has already begun at the birth of our Lord on this Christmas Eve.

A closing thought: Yes, there has been another year of sports on TV and controversies about athletic pay. Here in Iowa where I live, I observed that we have a refreshing sports story. A young girl, Blair Smith, lost her hair amidst increasing doses of chemotherapy. Her entire body was weak after spinal taps and other results of the cancer diagnosis. She stood near at the window of the hospital overlooking the football stadium.

> One Saturday, a crowd of 65,668 at Kinnick Stadium turned in their seats after the first quarter and looked up to wave to Blair, atop the adjacent University of Iowa Stead Family Children's Hospital. Her dad, James Smith, did not fight back his tears. "This is an amazing thing that all the fans are doing for the kids," he said.

As I read more stories online about this phenomenon, the practice of fans and the waving to children standing behind the hospital glass windows, points to new life and relationship between Iowa football and children in need of help young kids — even *if they are sick.* The news report concluded, "No football program in the nation [then] treats sick kids quite like Iowa!"

I believe this same spirit of caring, nurturing, and pointing people to new life is present right here in our church on this Christmas Eve. It is here all year around among the Christians here in our congregation. Merry Christmas!

Amen.

Works Cited

- "Brubaker" *AMC: DirecTV.* November 2019.

- Keck, Leander. Editor. *The New Interpreters Bible.* Volume IX:

- Luke John. Nashville, TN: Abingdon Press. 1995.

- *KWWL News* at 6:00 p.m. 12.01.19

- Vinson, Richard. *Smyth & Helwys Bible Commentary: Luke.* Macon, GA: Smyth & Helwys 2008.

Growing In Wisdom

He said to them, 'Why were you searching for me? Did you not know that I must be in my Father's house?' But they did not understand what he said to them. Then he went down with them and came to Nazareth, and was obedient to them. His mother treasured all these things in her heart.

And Jesus increased in wisdom and in years, and in divine and human favor. Luke 2:49-52

"Miss Millie" [African American Matriarch lady], taught elementary Sunday school in inner city congregation located in a rough neighborhood. She was a retired cafeteria worker. One time she "stunned me" in saying that sometimes she tells young teenagers to go to the Jehovah's Witness Fellowship. I was shocked! I protested, "That group does not confess Jesus as Messiah, nor do they believe in the Trinity and many other traditional teachings of the Christian church." Miss Millie persisted. She pointed out how in the streets of our city neighborhoods, there are drug gangs and the radical offshoot Muslim groups. Given the choices of gangs, and radical extremist groups, and the Jehovah's Witnesses (JW), she opted for the Jehovah's Witnesses. At least those young people would be clean and not into killing. When all the bad choices were presented, Miss Millie said she would go with the JW group. But this should give the Christian church more incentive to be more aggressive with its outreach efforts in urban areas. For now, there are young groups of impressionable young African American people wondering the streets looking for something to "join" so they can feel like they belong to something!

We live in days when we still see occasional stories about college fraternity hazing, which often results in hurting those young people who are pledging. They still want to belong a larger community who provides meaning in life. Unfortunately, the hazing portion often comes with acceptance into such groups. I am one who believes that

Christian campus ministry groups are a good idea at any college campus, even if the group is not of our denomination or is an ecumenical or cross denominational group. Quite often it is from such experiences that future missionaries, clergy, and other church leaders emerge and wish to share the vision of how God has met them in their discipleship journey.

In our gospel lesson today, we have Luke's unique story about the twelve-year-old Jesus. Luke is the only gospel that has any stories of Jesus as a boy. Matthew 13:55 indicates that he is Joseph the carpenter's son. The Greek word of *tekton* is used. This literally means "artisan of wood." It could mean "carpenter, craftsman, or general contractor" as related to wood products. The text says every year the family went to Jerusalem to the festival of the Passover as the temple.

In Luke's gospel, the "temple" is good and God remains present there. Luke's gospel began at the temple with the story of Zechariah and the prediction of the birth of his son John the Baptist (Luke 1:8). Luke ended in the temple with the disciples praising God there (Luke 24:52). Luke's gospel would be in agreement with the prophets Haggai and Zechariah who believed that God does great things for those who worship and respect the temple.

In many church magazine articles there has been discussion as to whether the church is the *building* or the *people*. Luke might argue it is both! The church remains a safe place in the eyes of most people in the community to drop off a loved one at a twelve-step, grief support, or some other small group gathering. The church building is usually kept up in terms of the lawn, exterior, and snow removal. The church building serves several such purposes in many communities. In fact, there are communities where the church itself does not have an active worship service on Sundays but is used as a meal site or soup kitchen for the neighborhood people in need. Church basements have been used as a place to store used clothing and other household items for either a rummage sale or to be sold at a small donation price. Luke in Acts still believed that God could do effective ministry in church buildings regardless of their history.

In our modern days of interfaith dialogue with other religious belief systems, some churches have even shared their worship space with other religious communities who have recently migrated to the United States, and retain their belief system from their native land.

While they were celebrating the Passover, the twelve-year-old Jesus engaged in questions and answers with the teachers in the temple. The root Greek word for "teacher" is *didaskalos*, where we get the term "didactic," meaning one who conveys instructions and moral observations. Some scholars have suggested that this was Jesus' confirmation or "Bar Mitzvah" But the text does not specifically say this. However, it is reasonable to assume that his family did follow that Jewish tradition of raising children in the wisdom of the faith.

Somehow Jesus' parents lost track of him as they travelled home. The assumption is that he was with extended family or kinfolk. It took them a day to figure out that he was not with them. They had to walk back to Jerusalem. They were in the city for three days looking for Jesus. Today, he would be a "missing child" and his parents might be turned into social services for not monitoring their boy properly. In our times, he might be a *"Home Alone, Part 5"* movie. The parents found Jesus and he was indeed with the teachers in the temple. They asked why he alarmed them. They were searching with great anxiety.

Jesus claimed he must be about his Father's house or affairs. This raised the question of who was Jesus' father — after all, if Jesus did anything wrong or committed any property damage, Joseph would still be held liable. At age twelve, Jesus already had a sense of "mission" in his life. I think this is hard for many of us to comprehend because many twelve-year-old children in our country are still growing and getting to know their own feelings and ideas — not selecting an occupation.

The other idea this text raises is that God has given the people a mission in our lives for however long we are here. They are a gift to us if they are with us. In our text, Mary pondered all these stories. She would one day see her son die on the cross for the sins of humanity. He would have been about thirty-three years old when he dies. Meanwhile, it is her task to help her son grow in wisdom while he was in his parents' midst. Death would not be the final word, but new life in the resurrection.

Today, what sort of wisdom are we imparting to people who come into our doors at our local church? I like to believe that we teach the basics of the Bible, our church doctrines, and catechisms as well as encouraging Christians to grow as disciples. Our desire is they mature in their faith as they are led by the Holy Spirit. One practice I appreciated in a previous congregation I served in was the summer Vacation Bible

School teachers in each class gave their students their own CD of the summer Bible theme to take home and play while they are with their families. Sometimes, the Vacation Bible School theme CD remains in that household even when the student has grown into their teen years — and now has fond memories of what Christian faith can sound like in any time era.

Another question might be to ask if the church council or board of elders in any given congregation have enough biblical knowledge, lived faith experiences, and discipleship skills to share and carry on a dialogue with any younger person in our congregation? What would happen if church council leaders, church trustees, and power people within any given congregation were expected to have a working knowledge of scripture, our church's beliefs, and where they are found in scripture? Also, they might present practical examples of how our beliefs have served the church in the past and continue to serve our congregation.

What happens if a person says, "I am not a Sunday school or any other sort of teacher?" The best instruction is by example. How do we "walk our talk?" I once had a council member named "Wild Bill" who had a horrible accident while in a school chemistry lab. He was in the regional burn center for a number of years. He graduated late in high school and went to a local small college. But he was very grateful for his second chance at life, despite physical disfigurement. He was active in church, town council, and he ran a small business where he hired and trained people without any college or higher education. When there was a crisis in town, Wild Bill was there with his time and yes — his wallet to help out! He believed that Christians need to roll up their sleeves and pitch-in if they expect the church and the small town to survive. He is walking his talk as a disciple. Wild Bill may never teach Sunday school, but he and his business are good at helping people with ponds who have worries about bacteria, insects, and possible loss of the pond during dry weather. He negotiates with each family according to their needs. He does want to be known as a fair, honest business person. He does not need much advertising, as his business grows through word of mouth. Wild Bill is being the best Christian he can be with his business despite his setbacks in life. He takes his Christian faith very seriously and respects people of any church denominational background, whether he agrees with their beliefs or not, they are still part of God's creation.

Jesus increased in years as he grew up to be who God wanted him to be, despite only living thirty-three years. Today, as this year comes to an end, what new life does God have for each of us here our congregations? It is never too late to grow in our Christian faith as a disciple. As of late, since I do a fair amount of writing, I have had school mates from my past contact me. Usually, they wish to propose some sort of memoirs of their life or life experiences and seek somebody to help them edit and organize a self-published style book or something similar. I think in the back of my mind that these might be modern versions of the Apostle Paul in the New Testament who also spent much time (while in jail even!) doing writing and editing with his scribe. (Some think it was Silvanus or Silas). These personal writing projects provided new life — even for those who experience their twilight years growing nearer to their time here on earth, as their physical body becomes more limited. New life is what Christmas is all about. The white and gold parament colors reflect such new life now as they do during Easter, another season of new life.

To conclude: when I do home communions in the dining rooms of the older people in our congregation, quite often, I also say the Lord's Prayer. I am amazed to look out of the corner of my eye to see others who are not taking communion who are also saying the words of the Lord's Prayer. In fact, I have seen the nursing care facility staff members, pause for a moment to whisper the words of the Lord's Prayer during the home communion service. Yes, we still do have communities which cherishes our Christian faith. Let us never stop finding ways to help others grow in wisdom.

Amen.

Works Cited

- Newman, Barclay. *Greek-English Dictionary of the New Testament*. London, UK: Unite Bible Societies. 1971.

- Tiede, David. *Augsburg Commentary on the New Testament: Luke*. Minneapolis, MN: Augsburg Fortress, 1988.

John's Christmas Gift

And the Word became flesh and lived among us, and we have seen his glory, the glory as of a father's only son, full of grace and truth.
John 1:14

Imagine a person buying a book shelf, dresser, coffee table or cabinet from a big box store or off the internet. The gift in the box is now in the living room and needs to be assembled. Upon opening the box and dumping the contents out onto the floor, one might look for the written directions on how to assemble this furniture. To the shock of the purchaser, the instructions are written in French, Spanish, or German. There are no English instructions, but there are charts and pictures of the assembled piece of furniture or cabinet.

The new owner spreads all the bags of pieces of furniture, nuts, bolts, and screws all over the floor. Soon it becomes apparent that there are some missing washers, hinges, and some of the holes are not properly aligned. The new owner must now take the pieces and assemble the furniture based on the pictures and what he or she knows about a cabinet of bookshelf.

On this year of the Christmas season, John the gospel writer has a disassembled set of stories, traditions, and teachings to work with in writing his gospel. They are the same stories and teachings which Matthew, Mark, and Luke also had when they wrote their gospels. John had the right story and the right pieces of the life of Jesus. He just assembled it in a different way. Let us take the Christmas story as John constructed it for us in our community.

The Christmas gift from John is Jesus' mission for each of us here in our community to have life and have it abundantly (John 10:10). The Greek word for life is *zway*, which means not only a quantity of life, but a quality of life. That is Jesus in John wants us to survive and thrive! We get the girl's name Zoey and the word zoology from *zway*.

Let us explore how Jesus in John wanted each of us here in our community to have life: "In the beginning was the Word, and the Word was with God, and the Word was God. He was in the beginning with God" (John 1:1-2). This is a very different beginning to Jesus' biography and family genealogy found in the synoptic gospels.

During this Christmas season, the child Jesus who was born was also with God when God created the universe. Rather than taking us back to when Jesus was born in the manger with Mary and Joseph, John wanted us to know that Jesus is the same God who created the world and continues to create life here on earth. Jesus was here with God in the universe, even before Mary and Joseph existed. After Jesus arrived on the scene, John the Baptist proclaimed Jesus as the Lamb of God "who takes away the sins of the world" (John 1:29).

Just like the other gospels, John's gospel identifies "sin" as the real enemy that causes death. Jesus takes sin away as we have faith in him. Life is not always smooth sailing. So instead of a wilderness temptation, Jesus attends a wedding at Cana where they run of out wine. This is like forgetting the wedding cake at a wedding today. Jesus meets this family in an awkward situation where they face embarrassment and, he produces new wine or new possibilities. This is my favorite text use to in wedding homilies. I remind the couple that a long-lasting relationship does indeed have unforeseen problems which result in awkward and embarrassing situations in public. Couples must take what they have and work with it, as Jesus did.

As this applies to us here in our community, many of us may face uncomfortable or awkward situations in these times. There have been the days of the COVID pandemic, but the news has also reported a roller coaster of unstable economic and banking problems. Jesus takes what is available, even if it is hand cleaning water, and produces new wine. Jesus meets us in those less than comfortable family or group situations and points us to new life. This is a gift during Christmas season.

In John 2, early on in this gospel, Jesus rides into Jerusalem, and knocks over the moneychangers and merchants who are using God's temple as a place for commerce rather than worship. Matthew, Mark, and Luke placed this event toward the end of Jesus' ministry-which resulted in his crucifixion. John the gospel writer wants us to know early on that Jesus is the new center of worship. Jesus is the Messiah who brings life. Why? Because in the beginning was the Word and the

Word was with God and the Word is God. Jesus is the Word, or God in the flesh. He was born on this day (John 1:1, 14).

Then, later one night (in John 3), a Pharisee named Nicodemus came out to check out Jesus to see who he really was or if he was a fraud. Jesus invited Nicodemus into a relationship with him, not just knowledge about "Jesus". It is then, that Jesus proclaimed another gift in the John 3:16 verse, "For God so loved the world, that he gave his only begotten Son, that whosoever believeth in him should not perish, but have everlasting life" (KJV).

In John, Jesus wanted more for us than we knew about him. He wants us to have a relationship with him and in doing so we have eternal life and have it right now tonight. This is another gift of Christmas.

That is all good and well, but maybe our life is more complicated than that. Early on in John 4, Jesus visited with a woman at a community water well — or the local gathering place. She came when nobody else was there at midafternoon when it was hot outside. It was discovered that she had an awkward living arrangement with many men. Furthermore, she was not a traditional Jew, but rather a half-breed Samaritan. Jesus promised to give her living water that would lead to eternal life. The woman was not judged for past lapses in judgment. Neither was she shamed for the otherwise awkward homelife situation she returned to live in. She placed her faith in this Jesus and became a new person. Furthermore, she shared the story of how God's Messiah had now arrived. That translated into good news for people in every community, including ours on this day.

Today, whatever awkward family or life situation we may find ourselves in, Jesus meets us, greets us, and gives us new life that lasts for eternity. This is another gift from God in John's account of Jesus' ministry for us in our community.

Instead of a last supper where Jesus instituted the words of "Holy Communion" as Matthew, Mark, Luke, and Paul in 1 Corinthians offers, John came at it from another angle. In John 6, Jesus took five loaves of bread and two fish and fed 5,000 people. All who want to be fed are welcomed. Then Jesus declared, "I am the Bread of Life. Whoever comes to me will never go hungry, and whoever believes in me will never be thirsty" (John 6:35). In that time, putting a roof over a person's head and meal took half a day.

Jesus provides for our needs. This is also taught in the other gospels but here Jesus' gift to us is that all are invited to eat at his table.

There was even food leftover. This is another Christmas gift, that there was leftover food from the Christmas meal. There was enough food to live and thrive (John 10:10, abundant life!).

To return to John 2, if riding into Jerusalem and knocking over the tables of the merchants and money collectors did not anger the "power people" enough to get him crucified, what action did get Jesus nailed to a cross as he died for our sins and arose from the grave? John 11, has the answer. Jesus has the power to give new life!

Lazarus, Jesus' good friend, had died. He was three days in the grave dead! However, Jesus raised Lazarus from the dead. Jesus is the giver of life! This is what threatens the power brokers in Jerusalem in John's gospel. Giving somebody new life is indeed what got Jesus arrested, put on trial, and crucified. The last words of Jesus on the cross in John's gospel are, "It is finished" (John 19:30). Jesus was crucified on a cross as in the other three gospels.

Mind you, just like Matthew, Mark, and Luke, Judas Iscariot betrayed Jesus. Peter, the lead disciple, still denied Jesus three times. Again, these are the same pieces of the furniture as in the opening illustration, but simply assembled in a different manner. John reminds us that God has things well in hand. All of this was in God's plan so each of us here in our community can have life and have it abundantly. In John, this crucifixion is Jesus' hour he referenced in the gospel since John 2, in response to his mother Mary at the Cana wedding. When was this all planned? For John, God had things well in hand, "In the beginning was the Word and the Word was with God and the Word was God" (John 1:1). The gift of God watching over and caring for the people of faith has been our assurance since the beginning of the world. What a wonderful gift for this Christmas season — even after Christmas morning gifts under the Christmas tree!

Just like in Matthew, and Luke and implied in Mark, Jesus forgave Peter and recommissioned him to care for others in the church and community. This is another gift during this Christmas season…we all get second chances, no matter how badly we have messed up.

If an unforeseen illness, bad economic forecast, natural disaster or loss of a loved one happens to us, John's gospel invites us to lay the pieces of our lives out onto the floor and discover other and creative ways to reassemble our lives in the upcoming year. It is all the same events and teachings of Jesus, but sometimes we simply need to find new ways of putting our lives together as John does with the life and teachings of Jesus.

We are given the gift to be creative during Christmas. Jesus is born of Mary. Jesus will grow up to teach, heal, and lead us. He will die on the cross for the sins of humanity and rise from the grave three days later. This is most certainly true. This year we are all challenged to find new and creative ways to build our faith and grow as disciples in Jesus the Christ. He was here before the creation and is with us tonight here in our congregation.

A concluding thought might be like from the movie, "*A Christmas Story*" — little Ralphie Parker wanted a "Red Ryder Carbine Action BB Gun" for Christmas. A subplot of the movie was that before their dinner, the neighboring Bumpus dogs ran through the Parker family kitchen and ate up all of the family's Christmas dinner. So, the family sought out a restaurant to eat dinner, to only find a Chinese restaurant at night. They ended up ordering a Chinese "turkey" (Peking duck) where the chef cut off its head in front of the family. The kitchen staff then sang the "Deck the Halls with: Fra, ra, ra, ra..." It was a memorable family Christmas meal, though not the regular tradition. This might be an example of God working in an unexpected and creative way for a Christmas dinner. Today, God has been there with us regardless of whether the holiday events have gone as planned or not... And the Word became flesh and lived among us, and we have seen his glory, this is the good news of the Christmas season as it is all year long!

Amen.

Works Cited

- Bauckham, Richard, *Gospel of Glory: Major Themes in Johanine Theology*, Grand Rapids, MI: Baker Academic, 2015.

- DirecTV, *TMC* [accessed December 2022]

- Lincoln, Andrew, *Black's New Testament Commentary: The Gospel According to Saint John*, Peabody, MA, Hendrickson Publishers. 2005.

Epiphany of the Lord
Matthew 2:1-12

Epiphany Stress

It was one of those rough Fridays that one wishes to forget. Everything went *wrong,* from the car having issues on the way to work to the machines at work also breaking down. People were in a bad mood. The phone seemed to have only irate customers and vendors.

The plumbing at the workplace was not working properly. Some key people called in "sick," so the office and shop were both shorthanded. It was the day from hell! When closing time finally came, there was an accident on the main highway and traffic was backed up for miles! What will Monday bring?

Today's text is a passage that provides a reason to wake up and do it all over again on Monday morning.

- Isaiah 60 points to the realization that God remains in charge and points us to new life and hope.

- On this Epiphany Day, we can have confidence that we are not in it all alone. God is the one who transcends any natural or human-made catastrophe.

- Today's Isaiah 60 addresses people who have experienced disappointment and disillusionment of their homecoming to Judah or southern Israel after many years of exile.

  - A modern example might be an employee or business owner returning to the job or work station after several weeks off — only to find it a total mess. Nobody really wants to clean this up and start all over again. But they are more than willing to watch other people work and clean up. I have heard such stories when people returned to their place of work after being away during the pandemic.

- Isaiah reminds the people that God is still invested in them and their future.

- However, do not expect some supernatural lightening out of the sky or superman solution toward a onetime success.
- New life is a process. New life will be the community coming together and working together.
    - I was a reading a book by Ron Allen, a Disciples of Christ Theologian in Indianapolis, Indiana, who reminds us that we do have the holy scriptures, particularly the Ten Commandments. At first glance, one might wonder why obeying the commandments and "being good" is necessary? Quite often those who are wicked or bend the rules do just fine. However, if one wants a community that works together and respects one another's boundaries and family goals, these Ten Commandments are good community guides. If one wants tension, conflict, and distrust — then ignore the Ten Commandments (Exodus 20, Deuteronomy 5).
- Regarding the opening illustration, Isaiah 60 might suggest that somebody should brew the pot of coffee and get the room smelling good.
- Also take time to share stories about our weekend and past weekends that might have been good or bad. (I do this in catechism)
- Essentially Isaiah 60 is telling us to get over whatever black eyes or setbacks we have had and focus on the light.
- Matthew 2 takes a text like Isaiah 60 to suggest that such a light is found in of all places — in the manger of a Christ child. Foreigners or wise men from other countries seek this light out.
- For Matthew, baby Jesus is the Immanuel or God with us. He will save their people from their sins (Matthew 1:21).
- He will not abolish the scriptures they have cherished all of these centuries, but he will fulfill them in even a fuller way (Matthew 5:17).
- Restoration will not only be for the Jewish people but for all nations as they are to be baptized in the name of the Father and the Son and the Holy Spirit (Matthew 28:16-20).

- God is revealing his own self in the Messiah who was born on Christmas Day. The invitation is not only to repair and restore our own homes and businesses but to be a light to all of the world! (Matthew 5:14-16).

- The people of faith are called to be part of the solution rather than the problem, as twelve-step groups put it.

- Today's texts invite us to ask which messes or places are we called to bring other people to clean up? We are not called to save the whole world — just our corner first then maybe help the neighbor.

  - One of my favorite stories of a past church I served is where the pizza restaurants were all in competition with one another on the same main street. One hot, humid, summer day, a huge storm came and blew off the roof of a couple pizza restaurants. The employees of the restaurants all came out and helped their competitors with buckets, tarped over the roof plus mopping and cleaning up.

- In Epiphany season, this might a realization of where God was in that time of the horrible wind storms blowing off the roofs of pizza restaurants! Uniformed workers of all the pizza places working together on each other's roofs and covering their pizza ovens. [God was there in the pizza restaurants indeed].

- Isaiah's theology is that of a servant who meets us when we come back from a bad weekend, a messy last Friday, or piles of junk left all over the floor from somebody else (Isaiah 53:1-12).

- The good news is that God still claims us as his covenant people. God's suffering servant did die for the sins of humanity and rose from the grave three days later (Isaiah 53:1-12).

- Regardless of the messes we clean up — God still wants us to continue growing as disciples, while baptizing other peoples in the name of the Father and of the Son and of the Holy Spirit.

Epiphany moments can happen in the messiest moments of life is the basic message of Isaiah 60.

To conclude, imagine that the power goes off in a certain town due to an ice storm. The people are told it will take a couple days to put it back on. The principal at the local middle school says their building has a generator. The principal invites citizens to come in with sleeping blankets and floor mats if they want to sleep on the gym floor. Furthermore, the school cafeteria has plenty of "Maid Rites" (sloppy joes) and chips to eat and they will brew some hot water for instant coffee or tea. In the middle of an ice storm, where was God revealing himself? In the middle school gym and cafeteria. They were part of the solution rather than the problem. Our challenge as Christians is how we can be part of the solution rather than the problem — whether in Fayette and Clayton counties here in northeastern Iowa or wherever we live.

Amen.

Works Cited

- Allen, Ronald, Eugene, *You Never Preach in the Same Pulpit Twice: Preaching from a Perspective of Process Theology,* OR: Cascade Press, 2022.

- Walter Brueggemann, *Isaiah 40-66* (Westminster John Knox Press, 1998);

- Luther, Martin, *The Small Catechism,* Minneapolis, MN: Augsburg Press, 1979.

- Claus Westermann, *The Old Testament Library: Isaiah 40-66,* Westminster John Knox Press, 1969.

- *Sundays and Seasons,* Minneapolis, MN: Augsburg Fortress, [accessed: 12.15.22].

Baptism Of Our Lord Lived Out

And the Holy Spirit descended upon him in bodily form like a dove. And a voice came from heaven, "You are my Son the beloved, with you I am well pleased." Luke 3:22

In a colony on the continent of Africa in the 1900s, there was to be a baptism event in two families. In the first family, it was a nobleman and his family to be baptized. They were stationed in this African colony away from their home in England. Before the baptism service, the father made sure that the caterers were present. He made sure there were musicians, fine wine, and the guest list was complete. He wanted this to be the big event of the year in the community.

Over in the next province was a poor native African family who were also to be baptized. The father made sure that he dug a huge hole in the backyard behind his humble house. He was going to have some fruit and nuts for a meal. But most importantly, he had to have the hole filled with water by creating a "bucket brigade" from the river. When asked by the neighbors why he was doing all of this, he responded that he wanted to have a hole large enough to drown out all of his and the family's sins. He wanted their sins to be buried into the ground, so they may have new life.

Mind you, both the nobleman and the poor African native family in the province still had the benefits of baptism. But one family saw it as a huge community affair (this is not totally, wrong!). While the other family saw it as a way to have the sins of the adults and children all cleansed and buried. Both families were then parts of God's community of faith. But what do their respective baptisms mean in daily living?

Today, Jesus unites himself with the people who know they need forgiveness. However, John the Baptist says he only baptized with water. But Jesus' baptism would be water *and the Holy Spirit*. The Holy Spirit's presence is what separated the baptism by John the Baptist from that of Christian baptism. Many Christian churches baptize people in the name of the Father and of the Son and of the Holy Spirit. This distinguishes the church baptism from that of John the Baptist's baptism. That has been considered a proselyte baptism into Judaism.

Today I shall talk about the significance of being baptized into the community of faith.

I have a pastor friend whose church tradition does not practice baptismal regeneration or "infant baptism" as my church does. His church tradition is "believer's baptism," where one makes a decision to accept Jesus Christ as Savior and Lord before receiving baptism. I have read some of his sermons. He is just as sincere in his view of believer's baptism, as I am regarding my baptism as a sacrament view.

The concern in their fellowship is that many people decide to come forward and "give their life to Christ" in an altar call in one form or another. However, this decision for Christ does not translate into follow-up in terms of learning more in scripture or developing a "discipleship" lifestyle. While the conversion is sincere and valid — there is concern that it is not taken seriously. Therefore, the witness of the church suffers. People do not take Christians seriously if they do not practice what they say they believe.

The same thing could be said for those of us who follow the sacramental path into salvation. It gets back to the opening illustration. Both families are Christians. Their baptisms are "good." They are part of the community of Christ. But how serious is the commitment when it comes to witnessing and furthering the kingdom on earth?

Luke's gospel and the church confessions make a couple points about baptism in our text. First it is about repentance. Jesus joined those who wanted to change their ways or repent, as he participated in John the Baptist's baptism by water. This was meant to teach us to redirect our lives so as to serve only one God — in a world that suggests that we can have other gods or loyalties on the side. (*Contra*: First Commandment, *Exodus 20, and The Book of Concord,* "Large Catechism," 365.1).

Martin Luther said that we are to look to our baptism to drown out the "old Adam and old Eve" from our lives. We are saints and sinners at the same time (*Book of Concord, "Large Catechism"* 444.64-446.86, Hereafter: *"BC"*). The intent of baptism is to snatch us from the "jaws of the devil" so we may pass from the present misery into eternal glory one day (*BC,* 446.82-83) "If we wish to be Christian, we must practice the work that makes us Christians" (*BC,* 446.85).

Forgiveness and repentance remain with us daily or we can continue to allow the old Adam and old Eve to control us (about our necks, BC, 446.86).

An illustration might be that two young kids went to church camp. They learned a lot and enjoyed the camp. Before they left, they all pledged to be good disciples for Jesus Christ. All campers received a church camp T-shirt.

Back home at school, one student who liked to wear his church camp T-shirt around town was polite and helped out other people in the community. Another kid who went to the same church camp and wore the same church camp T-shirt tended to be a bit "stuck-up and looked down his nose" at other people. Both students attended church camp and both students had a church camp T-shirt. But which camper actually practiced the discipleship of the summer church camp?

In Luke's gospel, Jesus' mission was to "seek and save the lost" (Luke 19:10).

For Luke, baptism meant daily repentance and living out what we believe in response to what Jesus did for us by dying on the cross and rising from the grave three days later. Many Christians do pray, "Forgive us our trespasses, as we forgive those who trespass against us" (Luke 11:4).

The second point about Jesus' baptism is that it was of the Holy Spirit.

> *"And the Holy Spirit descended upon him in bodily form like a dove. And a voice came from heaven, "You are my Son the beloved, with you I am well pleased" Luke 3:22.*

This is a theophany in that God speaks to people. This will also happen on the Mount of Transfiguration on this upcoming Transfiguration Sunday in Luke 9:28-33. Exodus 3, with Moses and the burning bush, is another example of God speaking or a theophany experience from the Bible. For many people going to a retreat or church camp is a time of spiritual retreat and renewal where we experience God in a special way. For those who are church camp and retreat enthusiasts, they always invite Christians to experience God in a special way at one of our church camps or retreat center events. In fact, some people feel a calling to full time church ministry at such events.

So, what does Luke mean by being influenced by the Holy Spirit? For Luke, the Holy Spirit reorients us into a life of following God's divine purpose.

I once talked to a college professor about the summer school programs on their campus. The summer program is usually offered to orient or help catch-up students who did not have a strong academic background into the college. That professor impressed me very much. I was told that statistically, students who take the summer classes actually do better in their final exams and graduate with more confidence in the major they studied while in college. There is a certain "spirit" during these months that carries on throughout the school year.

In Luke's gospel, the Holy Spirit reveals, guides, and empowers Christians to become disciples who discover God's purpose in their lives and the life of the community.

Prayer and public engagement help in applying this to our Christian faith.

I was once working [on a doctoral degree] with an African American Baptist pastor who was working with his denomination of clergy who had no college education. These clergy worked in some very bad inner-city neighborhood churches. One of the patterns that this student's research revealed is how constant prayer and interaction with the families and broken homes within their communities was a method of doing ministry. Furthermore, this was how lay members were trained to be church council and elders within the church — prayer and interaction with the community of faith.

As we are grounded in scripture and our own walk with the Lord, we become models or as Luther calls it, "little Christs" amidst the contexts of work, school, community, and other places we find ourselves in as Christians.

The Holy Spirit acts through prayer and applying our Christian faith in our daily lives. We may not be perfect. The twelve-step community has it right when they say we are about, "progress not perfection." Our God is gracious and is full of second chances if we do not get it right in applying our faith. We live our faith one day at a time.

For Jesus, his baptism was of the Holy Spirit. This would empower him to face wilderness temptations, debates with foes and ultimately a death on the cross for the sins of humanity. Three days later he would rise from the grave. As we confess him as Savior and Lord we have eternal life. Only in Luke's gospel do we have a narrative of a Jesus who does ministry right up to the final moments of his death. He replied to the repentant thief who was being executed beside him, "Truly, I tell you, today you will be with me in paradise" (Luke 23:43). Again, while the body and mind may die, the spirit lives on unto eternity. This is always good news for people of faith of any age.

On Baptism of the Lord Sunday, we are being claimed to be part of the community of Christ that lives on unto eternity. The mind and body grow old, but the Spirit lives on unto eternity. Today, Jesus' baptism is in the Spirit. This Spirit is in us here at our local congregation wherever we are located.

To conclude, when I go to area nursing homes or care centers to commune with one of our members, a part of the service is that of praying. We were praying the Lord's prayer and there were other residents at the table who also prayed this same Lord's Prayer with us. These elderly residents were indeed ready to meet their Creator. I remain convinced that such core Christian teachings and practice is what we need to uplift our identity as people of faith in the crucified and risen Jesus as Christ. Another reminder to take away on this Sunday is, the mind, and body grows old, finally all we have is the Spirit of the crucified and risen Christ to sustain us in our latter days here on earth and unto eternity. This is why all Christians take baptism, communion, and discipleship teaching in the form of Christian education, or confirmation ministry so seriously. It is part of our identity as Christians. And lest you think I am repetitious or growing old and senile — I believe this is worth repeating many times in the pulpit here as we join other churches in pondering what type of future is the Holy Spirit directing us in the years to come.

This is also an example of how we are marked with Christ's baptism, even when we are homebound in a senior housing apartment community, nursing home, or any institution, in a hospice care, or any other place of restriction. The spirit that was with us in our early years is with us as we age and finally when we die and live on through eternity. This is the good news of the Baptism of our Lord Sunday.

Amen.

Works Cited

- Green, Joel. *New Testament Theology: The Theology of Gospel of Luke.* UK: Cambridge University Press, 2005.

- Tappert, T.G. *The book of Concord: The Confessions of the Evangelical Lutheran Church.* Philadelphia: Fortress, 1959.

Fidelity

Madonna wrote a song titled "Material Girl" in 1985. Due to licensing rules, I cannot print the lyrics, but I would like you to look them up. It talks about one seeing the light and always being right.

What kind of "epiphanies" have you had that have changed your thinking? For me, it is area of relationships and marriage. (Hence, Madonna's "Material Girl" song). Whenever I have a choice to preach a wedding text, I always select this John 2 text over the popular 1 Corinthians 13 text. Why? Because I think the Cana story is a more accurate picture or narrative of relationships and family. Finances and money are a factor in any long-term relationship. In the book of Ruth, the mother-in-law Naomi made network connections with Boaz, the owner of the fields, not simply one of the workers who might take a liking to Ruth. Madonna would agree with this observation I believe.

When I am told or it is insisted that I preach on the 1 Corinthians "love chapter," I do share details behind the text to the couple. That is, Paul is essentially refereeing a conflict between sincere church people over many issues such as the allocation of gifts, money, worship space and leadership personalities. The conflicts actually escalate. This is why Paul wrote another letter known as 2 Corinthians. This 1 Corinthians 13 text is a "time out" chapter between exchanges of hostile words to other people in the community. Paul was providing a recipe for the ideal loving relationship between all community members in this 1 Corinthians 13 text. I tell the couple that I may share tidbits of this background in my wedding homily. They are free to use this text, but I prefer the John 2 Cana wedding festival text instead. Some couples give me dirty looks. However, 100% of the time, their more seasoned parents do agree with my reasoning and even say "Amen" a lot, even though Lutherans normally don't respond in this matter.

I was once reading many books on "cosmology." That is, "the science of the origin and development of the universe." Do we have a reasonable basis or evidence to believe in a Creator God of humans? "Is it reasonable to believe in a God?" One of the strands of thought this question takes us to is regarding human relationships. Is the practice of monogamy, or being committed to one person as our life partner or "mate" natural?

I read a couple articles from "Huffington Post" and saw some science programs on CNN that argue that most animal species do not stay committed to one partner. It is about finding a mate who provides the best roof over the family's head and which mate can reproduce the most amounts of offspring? I saw this also on "March of the Penguins."

In many ancient tribal societies, marriages are of a business proposition to consolidate extended family assets. Perhaps the butcher's family is now married to the dairy farmer's family. Then both families can enjoy meat and dairy products. The notion of selecting a partner based on choice and feelings is relatively modern.

In John 2, it is reasonable that Jesus is attending an arranged marriage. That is, it was well planned by both the families of the bride and groom. Both families are merging financial assets with this marriage and the wedding ceremony more or less seals the deal.

Jesus and the disciples are guests. Some scholars argue that Jesus' disciples drank more wine and then there was a shortage. Why the wedding planners did not foresee a shortage of wine is unknown. It would be like planning for our local catering service to feed the wedding party, and nobody showed up to cater the meal...just somebody who had one of those 24-packs of bottled water from the local grocery store.

Who messed up? Was it the bride or groom's side of the family? Is somebody already being forgetful? Was somebody already just looking out for the cake and no wine? These weddings went on for about a week. Since there were no refrigerators or freezers, the food had to be consumed entirely within this time period.

Back to the question of monogamy being natural. Should one side of the wedding party decide that already the other person is not living up to their share of the bargain? Let's end this now. Should we find other partners who are more responsible?

In John's gospel, Jesus' mother asked him to help this family out. Jesus responded that his hour had not yet come. He was not taking direct marching orders from his mother, but he was not saying no, either. He respected his mother but yet had boundaries as to how far she could order him around. The couple getting married could learn a lesson about extended family there.

Relationships are full of compromise, meeting other people half-way, and factoring in what in-laws and other relatives suggest, again while not allowing them to control the relationship. This could result in later conflict if the results of decision made do not have the desired outcome.

Jesus then took the purification water that was used to rinse people's hands with and mysteriously turned it into wine. In John, miracles were performed as a "sign." There are seven signs in John's gospel. After this Cana miracle In John 2, there are six other signs or miracles.

1. John 4 reports the healing of an official's son;
2. John 5 has the healing of man who was ill for 38 years;
3. John 6 is the famous feeding of 5,000 people with the little boy's lunch of fish and bread;
4. Later in John 6, Jesus walks on water;
5. In John 9, Jesus heals a blind man from birth;
6. Finally in John 11, Jesus raises Lazarus from the dead, to show he is giver of new life.

Each sign points beyond itself as signs do. A modern example might be a stop sign that points to an intersection with cars coming from more than one direction. The red octangular sheet of metal points to a reality that other vehicles may use this same intersection, so the driver needs to stop and yield to other cars.

As there was an abundance of wine for all people, John's gospel suggests that there is an abundance of grace for all believers in Jesus Christ. No matter how much we have messed up in life, God has a future for any of us whose faith is in Jesus as Christ. And despite any past errors or bad judgments, the best is yet to come for this couple and other couples who might have baggage from negative experiences in relationships. It bears repeating that for couples with blended families who have made bad choices, or errors have occurred in their lives, the possibility of the newest and finest wine is very real if our faith is in trusting in Jesus as Christ. He gave his life so we may have eternal life (John 3:16). He wants us to have life and have it abundantly (John 10:10).

Jesus and the Holy Spirit have signs and ministries in our lives, but also in their own time. Like in John when Jesus was crucified in his time—not when he was pressured in the garden by family members. In John 18, Jesus surrendered himself like walking into the local police station and saying, "I heard there is a warrant out for me. Here I am. Quit bothering other people to find me."

What Jesus wants from us and for us is to be as committed to him and our life partners as he is committed to each of us here in our community. It is unconditional love as one form of grace. Like at the wedding party, yes errors and mistakes happen...but Jesus has plenty of the best wine or his blood that he shed on the cross for us to last us a lifetime if not eternity (Brown, 110).

All of the theologians I have read on creation, cosmology, and humans being committed to one person agree that while divorce is real and is not the end of the world, such monogamy separates humans from any other animal species is our ability to choose, to love, to care, and to nurture one another — even when it is not convenient. The good news is that Jesus loves us unconditionally — even if and when we fall short of the "Material World."

This epiphany reminds me that I am fortunate enough to have a wife who has stuck by my side since we were married 43 years ago. I am reminded that the wedding vows "for better for worse, for richer, for poorer, in sickness and in health, to love and to cherish, until death do us part," are vows which are not to be taken lightly. I remind couples that less than 20% of the marriage relationship is good times and parties. The other 80% is work, but it is work worth doing. If I am never asked to do a wedding because of this, then fine. An Elvis impersonator or local justice of the peace can give the couple what they desire.

This epiphany reminds all of us that if our wine runs out, regardless if it takes the form of loss: patience, money, goodwill, or we simply are in a rotten or crabby mood for a long time, Jesus' love — that is his wine — is abundant. "I came that they may have life and have it abundantly"(John 10:10). This is the good news in John's gospel.

A closing thought is that I once performed a wedding that was the first in one of my previous parishes. The couple wanted it to be a model of family life. They requested that we go to the city zoo and perform the ceremony under a tent at a rented zoo booth. They had hot dogs and hamburgers on the grill. Rather than asking for gifts, they asked that the guests bring their children and grandchildren to the zoo. All people were to dress casually in shorts, T-shirts, tennis shoes, and flip flops. The wedding couple themselves paid a group rate for the guests and their families. After the ceremony was over with, they told the guests to go walk around the zoo. "Take their children and grandchildren to see the animal displays. Then come back for burgers, hot dogs, and drinks for all." The gorilla in the next cage was staring at us! There was a sign stating not to feed the animals, but they looked hungry. What should they all do? We all went on with our day. This is one epiphany of what family is all about! This couple wanted a wedding event that demonstrated what they believed healthy families should do — take vows; then have the family walk around the zoo with their kids. When it rained for a while, they had a tent over their booth and all were invited to eat until the brief downpour passed over. This might be an example of a Christian family being faithful to both vows and family. It was just as much about family and children than the vows. I think many congregations have the same sort of common sense to show creative ways we live out our faith in with our families here in our communities.

Amen.

Works Cited

- Brown, Raymond, *the Anchor Bible: The Gospel According to John I-XII*, New York, NY: Doubleday, 1966.

- *KOKZ Radio Station*, Waterloo, IA; December 2023.

- McGrath, Alister E. *Surprised by Meaning: Science, Faith, and How we make sense of Things* ,Louisville, KY: Westminster John Knox Press, 2011.

- Polkinghorne, John, *Theology in the Context of Science*, New Haven, CT: Yale University Press. 2009.

- Smith, D. Moody, *Abingdon New Testament Commentaries: John*, Nashville, TN: Abingdon Press, 1999.

Epiphany 3 / Ordinary Time 3
Luke 4:14-21

Factory Worker's Son

Truly I tell you, no prophet is accepted in the prophet's home-town. Luke 4:24

In every community I have served, I hear one or two voices who proclaim something in the effect of, "We need to find ways to keep our young people here or get them to come back home with us." Upon graduation from Lutheran seminary a couple decades ago, I decided to "test" these waters for myself.

A small Lutheran congregation just one hour north of where I attended high school had a pastoral vacancy. The judicatory office sent my name there to be interviewed. I was elated with the possibility of going "home." Many popular songs have been written about "Hey it's good to be back home again" and other such songs. At the call committee meeting, I hit it off really well!

My high school played (scrimmaged, actually) football with these folks' high school a few times. I knew the restaurants, radio, and television personalities of the local (Flint, Michigan) area very well. Our call committee meeting had much reminiscing or recalling past memories, major events, and key people we discovered we were raised with — or even knew! As I got to know them, we knew the same local slang and sayings of the area. I had a father and a brother who worked for one of the local big three automobile factories, as did many of these people. A five-hour interview felt like five minutes! They all knew who I was! How exciting it would be to go home to be a Lutheran pastor and be able to attend home high school games again!

But a month later, the head of the Call Committee phoned me to say that they opted to call a Navy chaplain from near Boston instead of me. I was told that they all knew me "too well!" They could feel in their bones that I was "one of their own." The sobering reality is that they could not see me—an automobile factory workers' son, being their pastor! They could not see me as a "minister of word and sacrament" — I was too much like them and their blue-collar sons! They wanted an outsider that they saw as a seasoned world traveler to be their pastor. Quite candidly the call committee chairman told me, "You are not a pastor, but an automobile factory worker's son in our eyes." Welcome to the world of Joe's boy, the factory worker's son. Yet, other states have always welcomed to consider me to be their pastor in any place I have interviewed

Luke 4:24 says, "Truly I tell you, no prophet is accepted in the prophet's hometown." Jesus traveled away from home and did many mighty works. Jesus healed people. Jesus casted out demons. Jesus performed miracles. Jesus debated with very intelligent scholars of his time. He had survived the wilderness temptation of forty days and forty nights with the devil. Jesus had twelve devoted disciples, plus crowds who could hardly wait for the next profound, wise word from his mouth. *And then Jesus returned to his own hometown!*

Maybe Jesus got to "catch-up" on news from the "old gang." Maybe Jesus' mom cooked his favorite dish. Maybe old Rabbi Herschel who confirmed Jesus let him share a few words in the temple? Jesus rose to the occasion. He read out of the scrolls of the Hebrew Scriptures from Isaiah 61. He, Jesus was the Messiah Isaiah talked about. Verse 22 reports that the crowds in the temple were initially amazed and the "gracious words came out of his mouth."

In the case of Luke's gospel, Jesus' vision for community transformation as Isaiah 61 describes it did not agree with what the leaders of that community envisioned as the path to their future. This has occurred with me throughout my ministry. I am a back-to-the-basics sort of pastor and teacher who believes modern Christians need to become grounded in the holy scriptures, and the basic doctrines of the respective church tradition. I have seen the major problem as biblical illiteracy and people unable to identify with the basic biblical narratives that have shaped and formed the faith of past generations. This might get a sympathetic hearing from older members of any given congregation. However, the majority report at many churches I have interviewed with use terms from the modern church growth culture to articulate the vision they see for transforming their community. In my years of ministry, I have heard expressions such as: "transformational leader, game changer, vitality leader, multiplication ministry" and quite often the church groups want a dynamic leader who can "take us up to the next level," however they define.

The pastor who likes to quote John 3:16, Psalm 23 and learn the ten commandments, Lord's prayer, creeds and church versions of sacraments or baptism/communion rites is not the type of community transformation leader they envision, as they interpret the Isaiah 61 text (that Jesus read to the hometown crowd). A pastoral candidate can protest all he or she wants to about how the basic biblical and doctrinal knowledge obtained in this very hometown church as to what informs their vision for community transformation entails. Jesus read it out of Isaiah 61. However, in a consumer culture, people want what people want. This factory worker's son could take his vision elsewhere. The call committee responded, "We will take a pass!" Then they contacted the area judicatory and asked for another list of names to interview!

Returning to the narrative of Jesus at the hometown temple, they suddenly realized, "Hey that's no messiah…that is a factory worker's son. That is Joe's boy, the factory worker's son!" You remember, old Joe the carpenter … the one where he and his wife suddenly moved into town out of nowhere. We know him, I used to see him work in his dad's carpenter shop. He isn't anything so special! Joe's boy, hum… His mom had that "virgin birth" story that we quite never believed. He isn't any smarter than any of us. He did not go to University of Jerusalem or Rome State College. This is a local working-class guy like us — not a minister!

"Truly I tell you, no prophet is accepted in the prophet's hometown." Have you tried to be a good parent and give out good advice, only to have your children ignore you? Then the neighbor lady says the same thing and those same children listen to her! Welcome to the world of Joe's boy or the factory worker's son. Have you ever made a suggestion at work as to how things can be done differently and were promptly ignored? Then an outside "expert" says the very same thing and it is called a "stroke of genius." Welcome to the world of Joe's boy, or the working-class guy's son. Have you hung out with the same group of friends for years and given advice that seems to go in one ear and out the other…then a total stranger to the group gives the same advice and all of a sudden it is seen as "wisdom?" Again, welcome to the world of Joe's boy!

As a factory worker's son, or Joe's boy, you could walk on water! You could heal lepers and help others who will indeed think you are smart. But when you get home, where everybody really knows who you are, you may become invisible. These folks might have remembered seeing your diapers changed. They know that your brother and cousins all smoke, drink, and chase wild women. Maybe in some other town you are seen as a "wise leader" but here at home you will always be the factory worker's son. Your sister worked in the local store. Your other brother worked at the gas station.

"Truly I tell you, no prophet is accepted in the prophet's hometown." To use traditional Lutheran categories, there is both "law and gospel" here. The law is that familiarity breeds discontentment. We feel we do not need to listen to those who are closest to us. We tend to feel like we have heard all of this before. We want to hear something different from somebody else! We can do our best. We can talk to them until we are blue in the face. We can pray, cry, and emotionally beat ourselves up because this loved one is on a slow path of self-destruction. Again, they will not listen to us. They may even think we are "nagging!" How many of us here in our community have families who will never listen to us as we see they are headed for destruction or demise?

Finally, we must do what the twelve-step community advises, "Let go and let God." We give ourselves a break and hand it over to God. Our loved one may be so thick-headed that it would take being hit by a two by four just to get their attention! Be at peace. You are in good company. There are some people in his hometown whom Jesus Christ himself could not reach! We must let somebody else try to reach them. God will work in other ways. This is the gospel, or good news of the text.

Yes, the factory worker son did die on the cross for the sins of humanity and rose from the grave three days later. Yes, Christianity is a religion full of second chances. But the hard reality is that there are some people whom we will never reach despite our best efforts. The good news is that God will deal with them in God's time. The hard reality is that we may be more successful in our life's goals and mission somewhere else than where we consider home! Why? In our own hometown, we are still viewed as, "Joe the factory worker's son? Even Jesus Christ himself had this same problem. If any of us are faced with the same situations of loved ones slowly going down a path of self-destruction, not willing to listen to us, be at peace! Even Jesus ran up against this same brick wall. God will use other means to reach our loved ones.

To conclude, I once read of a popular psychologist-type author who reported that he wrote many articles on family conflicts and problems. He appeared on local radio talk and call-in programs. Around Christmas time, his family wanted him to come home and talk with their dad about his drinking problems and overuse of alcohol. The son was hesitant. But at the coaxing of the rest of the family, he tried to talk to his dad, who had then drank a few beers and a shot or two of whiskey. The dad shouted to his helpful son, "You were no model kid yourself you know!" The dad proceeded to swear at his son. For the son, it felt like a knife was being stuck into his heart and twisted. Giving this man advice is like what Jesus said in Saint Matthew — it is "giving your pearls to swine" (Matthew 7:6). All the family could do then was "let go and let God" and hope some other prophetic voice would reach the father. The reality of living in modern times, is that often we are faced with post-facts sort of people, which may include our own relatives. They do not want to hear or talk about medical information concerning any sort of addiction, be it alcohol, tobacco, or any other sort of controlled substance. They remain with groups of people in their own closed circles or echo chambers of sorts who tell them whatever they want to hear. Medical or biblical knowledge simple does not matter!

Sometimes, no matter how much we love or care for somebody, we are simply too close to the situation. They do not want to listen to us. We are not seen as any part of the solution at all. If you don't believe me, then ask Joe the factory worker's son.

Amen.

Works Cited

- Brueggemann, Walter, *Westminster Bible Companion: Isaiah 40-66*, Louisville, KY. Westminster John Knox Press, 1998.

- Chen, Diane G, *New Covenant Commentary Series: Luke*, Eugene, OR: Cascade Books. 2017.

- Tiede, David. *Augsburg Commentary on the New Testament: Luke*. Minneapolis, MN: Augsburg Fortress, 1988.

Rejection

Have you ever been rejected? If so, welcome to the real world. I once read about a discussion which was going on in church leadership circles as to how wise it is to "groom younger people for success." It might be more profitable to train them to handle rejection, because almost everybody must face unhappy times of being rejected sooner or later.

Statistically, in the USA for about the past ten years, many young people feel so rejected and like failures while going to job market interviews that they return home and live in their parents' basements. The counsel here in Luke 4 is "Don't give up." Let me provide some modern examples.

J.K. Rowling was rejected by twelve different publishers. Finally, one publisher accepted her writings about a character named Harry Potter. Her writings have netted the publisher who believed in her, 1 billion dollars.

Another example is a young man who tried to get into the University of California Film School. He was rejected. He started to work on his own productions. Finally, he was given a chance and produced the movies: *ET*, *Raiders of the Lost Ark*, and *Saving Private Ryan*. This was Stephen Spielberg.

At age thirty, Jesus was beginning his ministry. He was baptized by John the Baptist (Luke 3). After being baptized in the Spirit, he was tempted in the wilderness. He taught and healed throughout the Galilee region. This was a distant area, which is geographically located away from the more traditional practitioners of Judaism of that time. He was returning to his own hometown of Nazareth. Jesus unrolled the scroll of the Old Testament (Hebrew Bible) as it was laid out on the table and read portions of Isaiah 58:6 and 61:1-2.

We learn that Jesus was a devout Jew who was well read in the Old Testament (Hebrew Bible). We recall in Luke 2, when he was twelve years old; he was sitting among the temple teachers. This suggests to our congregation today that reading and reflecting on the Bible or the holy scriptures of the God whom one worships was a normative practice since ancient middle eastern religion times. How might we apply this today? Are the devotional booklets many congregations offer in their narthex or lobby racks sufficient for faith formation on the level which Jesus has here?

The message that Jesus proclaims from Isaiah, from God, is to preach good news to the poor, release to the captives, bring sight to blind, liberty to the oppressed, and proclaim an acceptable year of the Lord. Some commentators suggest that this is the year of "jubilee" or total forgiveness of all people.

How would people today respond to such a practice as forgiveness of all debt and sins every seven years? Such a practice is rooted in two passages in the Old Testament, they being Leviticus 25:8-38 and Deuteronomy 15:1-11. Imagine how different life might be if people of faith quoted these passages as often as ones related to possible same sex relationships in the same book of Leviticus 18:22 and 20:13? Imagine how this would impact education and home ownership loans.

It is obvious that Jesus knew his Old Testament holy scriptures quite well. At first, he was well spoken of as the "home town" hero returning. However, Jesus' reference to the healings of Elijah and Elisha who healed Gentiles or non-Jews resulted in anger from the hometown crowd.

A modern example might be a sports hero who went to Central High School and returned home after he had made it big in the professional leagues. Upon return to Central High School, the crowd may think they have "exclusive rights" to their sports hero's fame. Instead, he or she announced that they will also start a sports clinic at the rival school of Northern High School. The hometown hero would donate money for the athletic program at the other Southwestern High School and accept a coaching job at Western High School. The people at Central High School would be very angry! They believed that their hometown sports hero should exclusively serve them and their school system. However, Jesus believed he was following the words and practice of such prophets as Elijah, Elisha, and Isaiah.

One canon critical scholar I am presently reading (Brevard Childs) suggested that when the Hebrew Bible cites the prophets, this is not to be viewed as the history of the community's reflection of how their past developed into the historical biblical literature that finally made the cut into the final edition of the biblical canon. No, the prophets were viewed as a direct voice and revelation from God! To ignore the prophet, in this case Isaiah, was a serious matter. It did not matter whether the hometown crowd appreciated Jesus reading the prophet Isaiah scroll, these were God's words. The listener is free to take them or leave them. Once shared and received, the crowds no longer have the possible excuse of pleading ignorance of God's word when spoken by the prophets. (Brueggemann, Childs, 18-19)

If Jesus sincerely believed that he was fulfilling the words of the prophet Isaiah that were directly from God, then the hometown crowd was not only rejecting Jesus the hometown son, but the very command of God's words. Is this the same God whom they worshiped in the synagogue on that sabbath day? Before we judge too quickly, might there be people in modern Christian churches today who listen to the Bible being read and simply ignore it or the words symbolically go into one ear and out the other ear, without having any impact on the inner being or soul of the person?

If a person such as Jesus cared for their hometown neighbors, friends, and extended family, this rejecting of the reading was not only personal, it probably felt like a gut punch that these people were rejecting God. This is not a new phenomenon, the people rejected God's words and warnings from God's leaders and prophets as far back as Joshua 24 when they were warned that they were never to serve more than one God. (Brueggemann, Childs, 113)

In Luke's gospel, Jesus' mission was to "Seek and save the lost" (Luke 19:10). This means a universal mission, not just to the immediate people of Israel. Jesus went and preached to them first.

Luke-Acts was written to a second generation of Christians who wonder where they fit into God's plan of salvation. The first generation of apostles has died. The Second Coming has not arrived. So Luke-Acts answers the question, "Is God active in our midst today? And if God is still active, where?" Luke's response is that God is working on bringing the kingdom of God to the whole world, not just one local area, one school system, or one nation. It is for this reason that Jesus was rejected in his hometown in Luke's gospel.

Another example might be, since I am a Michigan fan, while living in Ohio for many years, I wore the Michigan colors. But when asked about my not rooting for Ohio State, I would reply, "I will root for whoever will win for us in the Big Ten Conference in the bowl games. This could be: Indiana, Penn State, Minnesota, Iowa, or yes Ohio State or Michigan." Ohio State fanatic fans did not like that response. I told them, "I am a Big Ten enthusiast and I will root for the team that could win for the Big Ten Conference." This is sort of what Jesus was doing... he was looking out for a broader group of people than those in Nazareth or Columbus, Ohio, or even Ann Arbor, Michigan. In my current location Iowa City, Iowa, the home of the Hawkeyes, I continue to support all Big Ten teams who show promise to win the conference championship.

As this applies to any congregation, we must always look at the broader community, or beyond that of our own immediate neighborhood. Jesus' mission in Luke is to "seek and save the lost" (Luke 19:10). This might be a challenge to people who have not lived in any other geographical area then the one they were born and raised in since childhood.

So how might this apply to our Christian discipleship journey here in our local congregation today? Don't give up! Hang in there. Be persistent. In terms of rejection, if we believe God has a vision or mission for our lives, we do not allow others to detract us or to discourage us — even if they reject our mission.

In Jesus' case — not only did his home town reject him, but they wanted to push him over the cliff. This would not be his first trial such as the wilderness tests with the devil in Luke 4, nor would it be his last. He died on the cross for the sins of humanity and arose from the grave three days later. In Luke's gospel, Jesus' last words are "Father forgive them, for they know not what they do" (Luke 23:34). Jesus continued his mission to seek and save the lost, as well as prayed to God right down to his dying breath. As a result, he was also able to bring a repentant thief, who was crucified beside him into paradise (Luke 23:43).

During the Epiphany season, the question we might ask is what mission God has placed us on this earth to do-even if it results in many rejections from people we may respect! In a television Reelz special, actress Elizabeth Montgomery spent years trying to earn the respect of her then famous movie star father Robert Montgomery. Her father never recognized the fame of his daughter in her highly rated television series "Bewitched" as a successful acting career. Despite her constant pleas for his blessings and affirmations, it took years for her father to appear on the "Bewitched" television set. This might be another example of how God meets and molds our faith through such experiences during Epiphany.

While attending a small state college, one of students in my college management class was rejected from the teacher education program at the college. He had a speech impediment. The teaching education faculty thought that students would mock him if he was in front of a classroom of ill-mannered students. Also, his peers might wonder about his ability to instruct with such a speech impediment. By biblical standards, Moses could not have gotten into this teacher education program. The student went into the management program, and is now a trainer and instructor for computer, sales, and publishing companies.

Probably any of one us can probably recall a story of a child who ignored his or her own parents' advice on something, but will listen to the next-door-neighbor's words—who gives the exact same advice. In this case, familiarity breeds discontent. Rejection is a part of life here.

On this Epiphany Sunday, when we are rejected, if we believe in our calling or mission, then "don't give up." God will find a way to open a door or window, possibly in some unexpected way. If Nazareth or Jerusalem type of location rejects us, there are always other Galilee regions who might be more receptive and responsive to our words of wisdom. Also, possibly, it may be wise to have any form of modern instruction, mentoring, or education might be well served to have a rejection and failure component built into its requirements for successful completion of the program.

To conclude, Jimmy Denny was manager of the Grand Ole Opry in Nashville, Tennessee. A tired truck driver came off the road to sing one performance for the Grand Ole Opry stage. Jim Denny told him not to quit his day job – he advised him to go back to truck driving. He had no talent. The young man left and went elsewhere. He did not give up. That driver was Elvis Presley — the rest is history. Rejection is just as much a part of life as success. Also, let us never forget that some people are never going to be satisfied. Even Jesus Christ himself would not make them happy! Just ask the home boy from Nazareth.

Amen.

Works Cited

- Brueggemann, Walter, Childs Brevard S., *Old Testament Theology: Canon or Testimony,*Minneapolis, MN: Augsburg Fortress, 2023 edition.

- Carroll, John T., *The New Testament Library: Luke*, Louisville, KY: Westminster John Knox Press, 2012.

- *Dynamic Preaching,* Margate, NJ, n.p. January—March 2019.

- Matera, Frank J., *New Testament Theology: Exploring Diversity and Unity,* Louisville, KY: Westminster John Knox Press, 2007.

- Reelz television series [accessed; 04.17.23].

Epiphany 5 / Ordinary Time 5
Luke 5:1-11

Sent To A Calling

When they had brought their boats to shore, they left everything and followed him. Luke 5:11

How do you know you are sent on a "calling" from God? In Luke, one does not have to leave their occupation to also follow God's calling. In Luke 3, John the Baptist did not tell the multitudes, soldiers, or tax collectors to quit their jobs. He told them to be fair and humane to the people they worked with in their lives. Yet, there are those like Peter, John, and James who did quit their jobs to follow Jesus. What might be modern examples of the first case?

A patient arrived at a certain clinic for therapy and requested another therapist because she thought the previous therapist treated her like a "billing unit" — not a person. The woman was divorced and lived in a trailer with her ex-husband. Across the trailer court lived her daughter who had four children from four different men. This woman was on some form of Medicaid but worked part time to keep the family going. She hurt her foot and was in therapy. The new therapist recommended a ten-week treatment. As the therapist worked with the woman, the patient shared her personal problems and issues as the therapist listened, but did not judge her. If the woman skipped a week of her therapy, the therapist called her to see if she would reschedule the appointment or not.

The new therapist could not solve her patient's problems at home. But she could treat the patient in a humane manner as if this were her relative and get her back to full use of her foot.

This second therapist believed she was sent on a calling to "heal people" of physical ailments. She did not judge them, nor did she try to solve all of their personal problems at home. This is an example of living out the "call" in Luke's gospel.

In Luke, Peter, James, and John had endured a bad day of fishing. There was speculation as to whether the Sea of Galilee was all "fished out," or it was simply a day when the fish were not biting. Jesus went out onto a boat to teach. He had to be sitting as he taught because standing too long would tip the boat over. He instructed Peter, John, and James to put their boat out into the deeper water again and try to catch some fish. Peter whose other name was "Simon," protested but then did what Jesus instructed them to do.

This time, they caught fish...in fact, it is so many fish they had to signal other boats in the Sea of Galilee to help them gather the fish. Peter recognized that this man named Jesus was no ordinary teacher. Peter called him, "Master."

In the days of the New Testament, masters were power people that commanded and ruled over others with coercion. The Greek Word *epistata* or master appeared six times in the New Testament, all in Luke's gospel. This Greek word of *epistata* is the root of the modern philosophical word, "Epistemology:" This is the science and methods of the basis or grounds of what is defined as "knowledge."

Luke's gospel wished to shift the meaning of the term "master" into practices of: healing, deliverer, service, loyal follower, and a fear for that which was divine or a "God" of creation. Whereas in the broader Roman Empire context, the basis for knowing and methods of truth were forced coercion, holding power over other people's heads in the ruling classes. But Jesus' discipleship would be one of a lifelong learner...one always can grow in their faith in God.

Why do people sin or do wrong? In Luke, they need to be taught more. We see this in Jesus' last words on the cross as he was dying for the sins of humanity. While dying on the cross Jesus prayed to God, "Father forgive them for they know not what they do" (Luke 23: 34). In reference to Israel's history, this is unlike the Egyptian taskmasters of times past in Exodus (Exodus 11:1; 5:14). For Luke, not following Jesus was similar to returning to the bondage to brutal taskmasters as in the book of Exodus. Immediate rewards of good food and splendid architecture, also carried with the bondage and slavery of helping to uphold this evil empire.

So Peter, John, and James leave their nets and follow Jesus. It is contested as to whether they did mission work full time or did they return home to do some occasional fishing? Their first calling was to follow this new master of: healing, deliverance, loyalty to a divine God.

As this might apply to the opening illustration, the second therapist did not simply do the minimal work to be done in healing for the purposes of making the patient another "billing unit." Rather she listened and worked alongside this woman the best way she could so as to be a listening ear that did not cast judgment. Many problems persisted, but the therapist sought to assist in a restricted area of the woman's foot issues. This might be a cue for any congregation not to feel obliged to solve all of a given family or community's problems, but identify one area in which the congregation can be of assistance. Helping local school meal programs, making quilts to be sent to needy people overseas, and fundraisers for a local person's medical bills might be examples where Christian congregations seem to do particularly well. This is part of the calling of a given church wherever they are located be it a rural, urban, or suburban community.

The whole "call phenomenon" is also the point of this text. There are callings one is sent on that have a "theophany" experience to them. Other biblical examples include: Moses having to remove his shoes in God's presence (Exodus 3); Gideon beating wheat when an angel appeared to him in Judges 6, and one of the lessons of Isaiah 6, in the temple where the prophet exclaimed, "Woe is me for I am lost, a man of unclean lips."

But then in Luke 5:27-32 Levi, a tax collector, decided he was called to follow Jesus and invited the disciples and other Pharisee friends for a meal. Legend has it that Levi was renamed "Matthew," who wrote the Gospel of Matthew.

In my own personal experience in the fall of 1981, I received a phone call from the recruiter at a Lutheran Seminary in Columbus, Ohio. He was driving up I-75 to visit family. I sent him a letter of inquiry on one of those old small, manual blue typewriters in a small case where you had to change the ribbon. The seminary recruiter told me to meet him at the small restaurant at the Mall on 13 Mile Road and I-75. I did, and he took a napkin and drew out a program for me to go to their seminary. He paid for the pie and ice cream. Apple pie and coffee was my "theophany" experience on that day in the shopping mall restaurant! And, the next time my wife and I drove out of state, our old 1979 Chevy Nova stalled out in Columbus, Ohio, so I took that as a message from God to go to this Lutheran seminary. (I wish I was like Isaiah and prayed, "I am a man of unclean lips." But I used "not so godly language," as I kicked the tires of the 1979 Chevy Nova...we later got a Honda Civic, which angered my big three auto worker family).

Today, Luke wants us to consider if God is sending us on a call that does more than simply do a job for the day and go home. Maybe we are called to make a difference in people's lives in some way here in our counties in our state. Jesus calls his disciples. They would be life-long learners. Yes, they would slip up. In Luke's Gospel, Jesus simply reminds them to "learn from their mistakes and move on." This is how being sent on a calling is defined in Luke's Gospel.

With the above said, sometimes a calling can be quite costly. In the case of Luke 4, Jesus cited the prophet Isaiah 6. The prophet was a willing, enthused person who accepted God's calling — good and bad points included (Isaiah 6:8). The prophet associated with both the common working people, as well as the rich and powerful in Israel. He had a good working knowledge of the internal and outlying po-litical challenges in Israel. He took his calling seriously. Israel was at the crossroads of their history and the prophet wanted to make the leadership aware of the hard choices ahead, which may or may not compromise the nation's core values as a covenant people.

Jesus read the portion of Isaiah where the prophet speaks of a new covenant, transforming people's lives, being anointed with God's Spirit, and restoration of God's people. The prophet outlasted four kings of Israel.

However, legend says the wicked King Manasseh grew weary of Isaiah's harsh words of judgment. He was an evil king who practiced infant sacrifice. Yet, the nation tolerated Manasseh due to the econom-ic prosperity during his reign. Manasseh had Isaiah executed by fas-tening his body between two wooden planks, then having the prophet sawn in half. Manasseh's name is but a listed footnote in the Old Tes-tament whereas Isaiah's words and fame are read every Advent and Christmas season throughout the world.

During Epiphany season, another question to wrestle with is where God was revealing a calling to both individual Christians and con-gregations. Which cause or reason to carry on with life amidst darker winter days was worth dying for to glorify God? Have western Chris-tian churches simply outgrown the thought that we may be called upon to make the ultimate sacrifice for our calling as Isaiah did under Manasseh? Jesus had the ultimate cause to die on the cross for the sins of humanity, so he could defeat sin, death, and evil. Is there anything within the Christian religion that is worth making such sacrifices? The answer to that question may reveal a certain light in any darkness as to where God is revealing to us to grow in our Epiphany faith.

To conclude, "Buck" was raised in a household where his parents argued often. Back in those days, when couples got into fights, they threw pots and pans at each other. Police really did not want to get involved with domestic disputes then. Buck went out to the garage and found some saws, hammers, and wood. He found out he had a knack to work on wood projects and build benches, shelves, and tables out of wood. Buck was not a smart student academically in his local public school. His parents did not think Buck was the "sharpest tool in the shed." They discouraged him from going on to college. Buck went onto trade school and later got a journeyman's license as a carpenter. He started his own business — "Buck and Sons Inc.," as the family business. One winter when the work load was light, Buck's church asked for volunteers to build houses in Africa for their denomination's missionaries and a school. Buck travelled to Africa and found this to be a life changing experience. He was able to change lives. At age 64 or so, Buck did not travel to Africa because his body was aching and sore, so he needed pain medicine. As he was active in his church, his son decided to start a mission congregation and Buck himself had no regrets. He could lay down in bed at night knowing that he had lived the calling God sent him to do. It is my prayer that the people of both our congregation, may also get a flavor of this taste of fulfillment in life in this season of Epiphany.

Amen.

Works Cited

- Brueggemann, Walter, *Westminster Bible Companion: Isaiah 40-66*, Louisville, KY: Westminster John Knox Press, 1998.

- Carroll, John T., *The New Testament Library: Luke*, Louisville, KY: Westminster John Knox Press, 2012.

- Levine, Amy Jill, Ben Witherington III, *The Gospel of Luke, New York*, NY: Cambridge University Press, 2018.

- Metzger, Bruce, *Lexical Aids for Student of New Testament Greek*, *Princeton*, NJ, Theological Book Agency, 1969.

Kingdom Values

Today's gospel lesson reflects the ethical values of the kingdom of God in Luke's Gospel with the "Sermon on the Plain." Ethics are practices we should follow. Ethics are not always enforceable by civic law.

In the 1988 movie *"Working Girl,"* Melanie Griffith played a struggling secretary / office assistant who went to night school at Bronx College and was trying to climb the ladder of a competitive Wall Street brokerage firm. There men usually only wanted to use women for their bodies and ignore their ideas and abilities. Tess McGill thought she had arrived at the right position working under a woman supervisor, Katharine Parker (Played by Sigourney Weaver). Katharine was a smooth talker and welcomed new ideas. Tess pitched an idea for a corporate merger that she read about in one of the commuter papers while riding on the Staten Island Ferry. Katharine rejected Tess' idea. When Katharine had a ski accident, Tess was in charge of her townhouse and there discovered that her boss was in the process of stealing "Tess's idea" and pitching it as her own while reading on Katharine's computer. The movie grew more complex when Katharine's boyfriend Jack, played by Harrison Ford, fell for Tess. The ups and downs of the movie remind us that while stealing people's ideas at the workplace is unethical, it is not totally illegal.

Luke 6 is the text where Jesus preached his "Sermon on the Plain." Matthew 5 called it the "Sermon on the Mount" because Jesus, like Moses, stood on the mountain to share God's words to the people. Luke, on the other hand, had Jesus stand on the same level place where everybody else was standing — so as to appeal to the common person with his teachings. Scholars think both Matthew and Luke used a third author named "Q."

Luke 6 wanted to lead us to a vision of the kingdom of God or a version of the new Jerusalem, as was the ending song on "Working Girl" by Carly Simon. The heavenly kingdom comes down to join the earthly kingdom in Luke and other synoptic gospels in the Christian New Testament.

Luke's Gospel has the four beatitudes or "blessings" for those who are: poor, hungry, weeping, and are reviled because of their faith in Jesus as Christ. A modern example might be, I think the twelve-step groups have the right idea when it comes to practicing our faith when there are no easy answers. We are to be working in the solution rather than the problem.

So rather than complaining about hunger, how are we working to assist those who are hungry? That is why our organized church denominations have various funds, feeding, and relief ministries. That is why communities have homeless shelters. Our churches try to collect money for local benevolence. We even have area ecumenical ministerial groups who host food ministries. No, we will not solve all the hunger problems, but we are part of the solution rather than the problem.

The same is true for those who are sad, as well as those who feel hated for their beliefs. Many church service agencies can be one of the larger caring organizations that helps people in need. With that said, we can also be part of the solution with those whom we live and work around in daily life.

I feel comforted when I shop at our small-town grocery store and they still ask me if I need help to carry the groceries into my car. I feel comforted by the people in my life who will listen to me — even when I am not in the best of moods.

The community dinners and luncheons we have in our county are also great times for fellowship, which I do appreciate. I do visit with people from other churches as well. Even during the pandemic, many cars lined up in church parking lots to get meals and the people greeted one another.

All of these are examples of a community who works together as one way of bringing in God's kingdom. These are simply small acts of kindness. They are the opposite of the rough and tumble brutal world of New York City as seen in the movie "Working Girl."

Well, some, scholars ask why Luke added the four woes! Was he trying to scare us into heaven? No, Luke was trying to remind those who believed they were powerful and could control other peoples' lives (without caring for their best interests and well-being) that there will be accountability in the next life.

Luke's classic illustration was the rich man and Lazarus in Luke 16. The rich man was clothed in the finest of clothing and ate the most eloquent of food. He lived this life of luxury at the same time a poor man named Lazarus who was full of sores, and had dogs lick his wounds received crumbs from the rich man's table. Both men died. The rich man could not plead ignorance, as poor Lazarus sat at the gate, he thought he shielded himself from the poor — everyday! Death is the great equalizer! Lazarus is with Father Abraham and other believers from the Old Testament era.

The rich man was now in Hades, which is a place of retribution and torment. The rich man was still trying to use his wealth and power to boss Lazarus around by asking Abraham to make Lazarus cool his tongue with water. Later, the rich man wanted Abraham to send Lazarus to his father's house to warn his brothers of this torment and wrath. Abraham said they had Moses and the prophets. But maybe if somebody would rise from the grave to warn them, they would listen. Luke left the reader guessing, "Who might this person who rises from the grave to be? Might it be this same Jesus who is also preaching the Sermon on the Plain here in Luke 6?"

The "woes" were simply reminders that we all have to be accountable to God one day after death. This might be a modern reminder from Luke the evangelist that Christianity is more than a "get out of hell free" card. Christian discipleship has a certain responsibility that begins before and continues in the afterlife.

This sermon was preached to all people. One does not need to have special Old Testament knowledge, like in Matthew's Gospel. This is why Jesus preached it on a "plain" or flat land so all people could see, relate, and understand Jesus. It is also why he used common life examples that people from any ethnic origin might recognize.

Kingdom ethics here were to be a blessing by being part of the solution rather the problem. No, we do not have to be able to provide all the answers. We simply do the best we can with the spiritual gifts and abilities God has given each of us here in our congregation today.

Also, in Luke you do not have to quit your job to be a missionary, pastor, or professional church worker. From the days of John the Baptist, soldiers were told to remain soldiers — just don't rob anybody with their power position. Tax collectors can keep their jobs, just be fair to the citizens (Luke 3:7-14).

When it comes to the *love your enemies* part of the lesson — Luke means, "Don't fight fire with fire." We are to rise above name calling, and using the same evil tactics bad people use. We can still stand up for our safety and that of our families. Another metaphor might be we do not wrestle in the dirt with a pig! Why? Because the pig likes it.

This is why I am one who likes to write letters and email to companies rather than yell and get mad for any period of time at the cashier or front-line worker. In these times, I also send email and take surveys. In fact, I was asked to do a television Nielson ratings survey one year.

Finally, the text reminds us to be merciful that is we err on the side of grace and mercy when we are not sure of the motive of people who might hurt us (Luke 6:36). Our God remains a God who errs on the side of grace. The repentant thief on the cross aside of Jesus in Luke 23 might be one case and point.

Another example, was a young man in junior high school was trying to make an impression that he was a "tough guy" in front of his friends. However, he struggled in math. The math teacher sent a tutor to study hall to help the boy. The tutor was a sweet young gal with a bright and happy smile. Her presence "tarnished" the "tough guy" image the boy was trying to impress upon his friends. Who was working for and against the kingdom in this case? The boy should see the bigger picture of school was to get his math grades up — not make a good impression on his friends.

In Luke's Gospel, kingdom values were to be lived here and now. Once we are baptized (or converted), we are citizens of a kingdom where Jesus died on the cross and rose from the grave. If our faith is in this risen Lord, then we live by his example and values. We do not have to sacrifice an "arm and a leg," — simply being part of the solution rather than the problem here in the communities our churches serve in our state.

This is not always easy. During my first year in seminary our theology professor told us about the merits of living a life under the theology of the cross. Indeed, God meets us in our valleys, times of depression, rejection, and when the world sees us as being in last place on success ladder. In times of turmoil, where is God? God suffers alongside us as Jesus with the cross. I thought to myself, "What a wonderful way to explain God's forming and molding our faith!" But that same professor warned us that before we consider going further into the ordination process, remember that all theology is a "prescription for the church, not a description of it."

He reminded us that many medical doctors give prescriptions and pharmacy scripts, which are not often filled. If they are, often only half of the pills and recommendations from the physician are followed. Those patients are physically sick and often bedridden. With that said, imagine how difficult it is for clergy and church leaders who have given prescriptions and spiritual healing instructions for people's souls. Not all people are going view living under the cross similar to Isaiah's suffering servant or Jesus' crucifixion on the cross for the sins of humanity as a pleasant prescription. It may never be the description of the Christian discipleship growth process for many people. The church's task remains to live out the kingdom ethics in both word and daily practice. That is how we live out the "kingdom values." The Sermon on the Plain here in Luke 6 provides a basic playbook or nuts and bolts instructions on how to live out these kingdom values. The "woes" serve as reminders that all people are ultimately accountable to a God of grace, who still blesses people of faith who try to be part of the solution rather than the problem.

To conclude, in 1991, "Mike and Julie," a Jewish couple received a phone call from Larry, the Grand Dragon of the Ku Klux Klan in Nebraska. He took great joy in harassing new immigrants to the USA and encouraged vandalism on their property. He left his name and phone number and harassed Mike and Julie often. But Mike and Julie returned KKK Larry's phone messages with friendly greetings, caring words, and wishing him well for the holidays. One year, Larry became blind and became a wheelchair bound diabetic. Mike and Julie offered to run errands for him and help him in his house. Larry was so impressed that he converted to Judaism and became an FBI Informant. Mike and Julie responded to Larry's hatred with love from the God of Abraham in the Old Testament. This same God loves us here in in our communities in this year and the years to come.

Amen.

Works Cited

- Al-Anon Family Group, *One Day at a Time,* AFG, 1980

- Carroll, John T. *New Testament Library: Luke,* Louisville, KY: Westminster John Knox Press, 2012.

- DirecTV *"Working Girl." 01.25.19.*

- *Dynamic Preaching,* Margate, NJ, n.p. January-March 2019.

Epiphany 7 / Ordinary Time 7
Luke 6:27-38

God And Enemies

But I say to you that listen, love your enemies, do good to those who hate you, bless those who abuse you. Luke 6:27-28

This text is a tall order back in the days of Luke, as it is today. Yet it is part of the discipleship journey and had a parallel in Matthew 5:39-42. What might be a modern-day example of trying to apply this text?

An employee for an organization for whom the person has worked tirelessly to achieve the objectives operation for years was suddenly called into a closed-door conference room meeting at Friday about closing time. Up on the wall were two Zoom screens with unfamiliar faces wearing a serious facial expression. The executive director and human resources person were seated at the same table as the employee. The executive director announced to the worried worker that their position is terminated immediately. The organization was reorganizing and this worker's skill sets were no longer needed. They were to turn in both their keys and work badges immediately. There would be a three-month severance package if the employees agreed to sign a nondisclosure agreement, and to not discuss with this with anybody in public.

The employee reminded the persons in the room of the years of sacrifice and effort they made for this organization. They also reminded them they have a family to support and the need for medical benefits. The room was so quiet that one could hear a small pin drop. The employee looked to supervisors who had been friends for years and even shared family events with on holidays. They would not establish any eye contact with the tear swelled former colleague. The executive director seemed to be trying to impress the two faces upon the Zoom screen with words of harsh criticism for work performance, unsubstantiated rumors, and threats to call enforcement if the now ex-employee does not leave the premises immediately.

How does one deal with the "love your enemies, do good to those who hate you, bless those who abuse you" now? Such muggings have occurred in corporate, faith-based, and education organizations across the nation in recent years. Nobody's education credentials or work experience insulates them from such muggings! How does a person of faith in the God of the Bible respond?

When I find a text in the New Testament that I struggle with, I recall that the New Testament as we have it today was not finalized until 405 CE. The Bible of the early church was indeed the Old Testament or Hebrew Bible. Our psalm lesson for today is Psalm 37. I choose to interpret this Luke 6 text through the lens of Psalms such as Psalm 37 today. I qualify this by saying I tend to read all of the Old Testament (Hebrew Bible) through the lens of the Jesus as Christ event dying on the cross for the sins of humanity and rising from the grave three days later. This is not to say mine is the only way to read the psalms, as there might be other ways to read the psalms. I find comfort in knowing that the early Christians did have the book of psalms as a resource to reflect on the teachings of Jesus in Luke's Gospel.

Such a psalm is what some scholars (Creach, 179-182) call "imprecatory or vengeance psalms." Vengeance belongs to God. Vengeance is neither the right or responsibility of human beings. To hang onto the desire for vengeance for oneself is also a subtle way of mistrusting the God of scripture. Our Psalm 37 lesson confronts the unfairness of life head on! Good people often get abused while wicked people prosper. This is part of wisdom literature, even in the book of Job. However, the psalmist believed people of faith should trust in God's providence and justice. He went on to say, "Do not fret because of the wicked, do not be envious of wrong doers. For they will fade like the grass and wither like the green herb." The psalmist used a double strophe in each verse to highlight the reality of wicked doers, but also used two strophe clauses to underscore that such people would wither and die. Literary devises such as double strophes were used for emphasis without the use of modern underscoring, italics, or bold type as used in printed manuscripts today.

The psalmist went on to state what would be in harmony with our Luke 6 text, "Trust in the Lord, and do good so you will live in the land, and enjoy security. Take delight in the Lord, and he will give you the desires of your heart" (Psalm 36:3-4). This points to a belief in both

God's providence and sovereign rule over the universe, both good and wicked people.

As this relates to Luke 6, an opening illustration of even loving one's enemies was a tall order and counter-cultural in many settings. One is to trust in God's providence. In Luke's Gospel, we do see reversals such as the rich man and Lazarus in Luke 16, as well as the wicked tenants in Luke 20. Therefore, it might be reasonable for the employee in the above illustration to realize that God will one day come to "judge the living and the dead" as the Apostles' Creed states.

The calling for disciples in Luke was to rise above petty grievances, arguments, and people who perpetuated divisive situations. A modern example might be a person who dreads going to their in-laws' house for the holiday gathering every year. Why? Because certain family members live to argue and debate over anything from religion, politics, and sports to local school activities. These relatives like to instigate arguments over any topic and they grow even more obnoxious as they consume more alcoholic beverages. They will take the opposing view on any topic, even the color of the sky, for the sake of argument.

Luke 6 counseled the faithful disciple to avoid debating and arguing with such people. As some twelve-step groups might put it, "I don't have to attend every fight I am invited to." This is the spirit of Luke 6. Some people are simply not nice to be around and grow even more mean spirited when challenged. No amount of logic, citing scripture, or trying to be reasonable will satisfy them.

Simply let them take their best verbal potshots at you. To exaggerate the point, if they want your plate of food, give them your desert also. While still maintaining healthy boundaries, it is better to avoid conflict with certain people that you know you may never satisfy. Meanwhile, in whatever way you can, let them know you still care and are concerned about them, even though they may retaliate with more foul language. At a family gathering, you can still be nice to family members — who also probably are aware of the uncomfortable situations.

This is a practical application of Luke 6 when it comes to God and enemies. The psalms would still permit us to place the offending person in God's care and will. For example, if the person gets into an accident on the way home due to bad decisions, it is their own fault and God will do what God will do in God's time.

The world operates in an economy of liability and credit. Christians are to err on the side of grace — even for those people who are less than compassionate, possibly mean spirited! Even to the point where we are not to try to find fault with other people — lest we too will one day have lapses in judgment. One day, we might find ourselves in the situation where we are an employer who must release people from their jobs, as what often occurred during the pandemic a few years ago.

We all need God's grace and forgiveness. This is why our basic Christian gospel message is that Jesus' death on the cross and resurrection from the grave is intended to apply to all who have faith in this Jesus. If their faith is elsewhere, then they will be delivered to that "false god" (Paul Tillich, *Courage to Be*).

Meanwhile, the pain and wounds from being fired from an organization or abused by a power person still do not go away. Psalm 34 counsels' people of faith, "Yet a little while the wicked be no more; though you look diligently for their place, they will not be there. But the meek shall inherit the land, and delight themselves in abundant prosperity" (Psalm 37:10-11).

Jesus, in Luke 6, provided the roadmap for the meek who will inherit the land, and delight themselves in abundant prosperity." Jesus said, "But love your enemies, do good and lend expecting nothing in return. Your reward will be great, and you will be the children of the most high; for he kind to the ungrateful and wicked, Be merciful just as your Father is merciful" (Luke 6:35-36).

One of the other realities that rarely is mentioned regarding "imprecatory or vengeance" psalms when pointed out is harsh texts such as Psalm 37 or 137 regarding God being asked to dash an enemies' little ones against the rock (Psalm 137: 9). How can a loving God answer such prayer requests? It comes back to trusting in God's judgment and providence. One has to assume that God sees a larger picture as he pointed out in the whirlwind to Job in Job 40-41.

One of the more animated discussions we had while I was in seminary was regarding the victims of the holocaust by murdering millions of Jews, political prisoners, and physically challenged people. How could their families even "think" of forgiving such atrocities? After much animated debates about the scars and wounds of the families, one proposed solution was while forgiveness might be difficult to offer the perpetrators of such atrocities, turning the people and situation over to God might be one solution. That God will deal with such people in God's time was acceptable to some people, while not others who simply questioned God's providence from the very beginning.

Earlier in Luke 5, Jesus added "woes" to the "blessings" in the Sermon on the Plain. This a reminder that there is a judgmental side of God. Again, Christians are not to be the ones who seek vindication according to Luke's gospel. The epiphany theme here is that God can reveal God's will in both the blessings and woes. Luke 6 wants believers to rise above fighting on the same level as those who can be seen as enemies.

To conclude, the 1999 movie, "Office Space" was a satirical movie about educated engineers and office workers who hated their jobs at a high-tech firm called "Initech." The movie highlights the dreary life of one Peter Gibbons who dreaded going to the daily grind of his job and doing the mindless paper work it entailed. Despite an epiphany moment at a therapists' office by Peter, the company continued its harsh treatment of employees. Initech's obnoxious vice president Bill Lumburgh made conditions worse, by bringing in consultants who had the nervous employees' interview to keep their own jobs. There were other subplots that occurred surrounding this evil corporation, such as demands for workers to give up their weekends to do more mindless jobs.

Peter Gibbons himself got into trouble regarding siphoning off loose pennies of money which translated into the missing of major amount of funds in the corporate books. There was also a twitchy, mumbling long-time employee named Milton who complained about his desk being moved and his red stapler being taken. Just as Peter Gibbins was about to go into work to turn himself in from his mishaps, the employee named Milton had hit his threshold of anger. He had his stapler stolen one time too often and then his paycheck discontinued. The Initech building was burning to the ground! One way to face up to the bosses at Initech, was the company building was burned down. One suspects it was probably Milton the who set the fire and who may now be living on a distant beach resort. Could this be one example of God's indirect judgement on an evil corporation such as "Initech?" The viewer is left wondering and drawing his or her own conclusions.

Both Luke and Psalms might agree that evil organizations might reap their own demise or punishment indirectly at some unknown time. This might be one serendipitous moment of God's judgment.

"Trust in the Lord, and do good; so, you will live in the land, and enjoy security" (Psalm 37:3).

Works Cited

- Brueggemann, Walter and William Bellinger, *New Cambridge Commentary: Psalms,* New York, NY: Cambridge University Press, 2020.

- Chen, Diane G., *New Covenant Commentary Series: Luke,* (Eugene, OR: Cascade Books, 2017

- Creach, Jerome D., Discovering Psalms: Content, Interpretation, Reception, Grand Rapids, MI: Wm. D. Eerdmans, 2020.

- Tillich, *Paul Courage to Be,* New Haven, CT: Yale University Press, 1959.

Transfiguration Sunday
Luke 9:28-43

Transfiguration Values

Now about eight days after these sayings Jesus took with him Peter and John and James, and went up on the mountain to pray.
Luke 9:28

What happens when the life narrative we have planned on, does not work out the way we had intended. This can be related to job, family, community, and yes health. It is in this time we need a Transfiguration values moment to look back upon.

Once there was an older couple that had some difficult decisions to make. Their adult son had been living with them for some years now and he was unable to keep a job. He was abusing their hospitality. Their pension and retirement looked to be tighter than what they had planned. Medical costs were going up as they looked further into retirement — not going down as they were told earlier!

They went away for a long weekend retreat to their church camp near a lake with other older couples such as themselves. It was a delightful experience. It was a weekend of singing, reading scripture, and featured speakers on spiritual growth. They talked with other couples about similar issues and problems. They vented their concerns about their adult son at meals. They stayed up for late night talks to sort issues out in their lives. Sure enough, other families had similar issues with both adult sons and daughters, along with tales of being responsible for the grandchildren as the parents are in no position to take over such responsibility.

As with other retreats, they enjoyed the outdoor food and campfire events. Simply being with people like themselves who lived with similar experiences of life foiled narratives made it a weekend they did not want to end. They may have wanted to build three booths there and remain, as Peter suggested (Luke 9:33). However, Monday morning arrived and it was time to depart back home.

When they were done with the long weekend, the older couple was able to put their problems and life in perspective and see things from varying points of view. They would have to give their adult son choices and stick to their boundaries. Twelve-step groups also practice this. They will have to do more pre-planning and look at options for finances when they consider retirement.

They drove home as "different people" with a certain peace of mind and happiness in their heart. This was their transfiguration experience. The problems of home were still there.

They had seen the glimpse of glory at the church retreat camp that other couples shared with them. This is an example of a modern Transfiguration Day experience. This is what God wants for us from this text on this day in our congregation.

Today, God wants Peter, John, and James, as well as each of us here at our church to see Jesus in a differing way than what the world wants to see Jesus — so we too can experience God in a way that will change our lives. The problem is the expectations that people placed on Jesus, as well as modern expectations we see being placed on God and the community of Christ.

Peter, John, and James — like many people of their time — sought a Messiah who would take away their problems, like now! They liked Jesus the healer, in a time when medicine was archaic and people died at a young age. They liked Jesus as the preacher who imparted wisdom and new teachings to them. They liked Jesus as a prophet who confronted the power people of his time. They liked Jesus as the one who casted out demons and rid the world of dark forces.

For many practical reasons, many religions would seek this from their leader. But Jesus wanted more for his disciples than these, though having a: healer, preacher, prophet, and exorcist. These are not bad qualities.

Jesus wanted his disciples to see him for who he really was. One year, on the Tyra Banks television show, they conducted an experiment. They had beautiful models who had many doors opened for them with their mere looks — get dressed up and made up to look like average-looking overweight women. These same women applied for jobs and other positions right alongside their beautiful counterparts.

The now average looking overweight women were totally shocked — how life was really like for those women who are not slim, thin, beautiful people. There was the realization that the people whom they work with and were liked for their looks and beauty were not liked for who they really were.

Jesus was showing the disciples who he really was. Jesus loves us for who we really are. Jesus was indeed the one whom Moses and Elijah of the law and prophetic traditions had predicted to come for the people of God. Jesus was showing his "transfiguration" or his change. He was getting more than the facelift that the models received on the *"Tyra Banks Show."*

Jesus wanted the disciples to see who he really was. The very Son of God in the flesh!

Jesus represents the prophetic tradition in Elijah in that he worshiped God alone. The wilderness' temptations in the desert proved this when he did not allow other false gods to detract him from his mission (Luke 4).

Also, like Elijah, Jesus had named and rejected false gods and experienced the wrath of both the government and religious authorities. He knew the pain of being right, and still being rejected and threatened. The couple in the opening illustration had probably talked to their adult son many times about job, family, career, and maturing as an adult — only to be rejected.

Jesus represented the tradition of Moses in that he would deliver people not only from superpowers such as Pharaoh, but from death and the sting of death. He would do this by dying on the cross for our sins and rising from the grave three days later (Luke 23-24). Meanwhile, Moses did have to deal with grumbling people who wanted to experience one miracle after another during their times of daily living. Jesus was also tempted to become a traveling miracle and healing show on the road. In Luke, his mission is to seek and safe the lost (Luke 19:10).

The mountaintop experience is a reminder that Jesus is who he says he is. Those who want to draw closer to him are invited to travel the journey of faith.

What did the disciples want to do? They were like many people. They wanted to stay on the mountaintop and have one mountaintop experience after another without going into the valleys, the hard times, and the struggles. They wanted to win the game without going to practice. They wanted an "A" on the test without studying and learning the materials. They wanted to have the perks of community, friendships, and family — without spending time with the community, friends, or family.

One time, two younger women who were about to get married were taking cooking lessons from an older, heavy-set woman who had sort of a rough demeanor and bad speech. The one, who was a more "proper," woman did not even like being around this older woman with the rough demeanor. She did what she had to do to be in the kitchen. The other young woman spent time with this older woman to learn all that she had to offer. She ate lunch with her. She treated her like an aunt or elderly relative with eccentric ways. She got to know about her family, plus her past and current problems. This woman really learned how to cook the quality meals that impressed everybody. Whereas, the other woman who kept her distance often asked that her friend write down the recipes.

The woman who got to know the older woman cook could walk out of the kitchen with a certain "air" of confidence that she knew what she was doing in the kitchen. The other woman had to rely on other people's recipes or simply use the microwave often. She was glued to her notes and recipe books. This was her choice. The other lady needed not feel guilty or take ownership of the woman who put in minimal effort to learn the cooking recipes.

Jesus wants each of us to have that feeling of confidence that he is with us during all of our hard times. This God of the cross remains beside us when we are not playing our "A" game. Jesus wants to remind us that as we have traveled down many difficult paths in life, that we have confidence to make it in many other challenges in life. Jesus wants us to feel comfortable going on any journey in life — knowing that he wants us to have life and have it abundantly (John 10:10).

The problem is that many people try to take the shortcuts or the easy way out. On Transfiguration Day, we are reminded that our faith values in Jesus as Christ is worth it.

We are reminded that in our daily ministries as Christians, there is no valley to walk through, nor no mountain too tall to climb, where we do not have the hope of new life. This is especially true when the envisioned narratives of life which we counted on, do not materialize.

At our local church, our response as a community of faith is to practice the gospel through the actions of our ministries here at church. This includes Christian education ministries, council, and community food ministries. We do ministries where we work, study, and live.

Transfiguration theology suggests that we will not have to *tell* anybody that we have a confident faith in God and our future. People will see it in our faces and the lives we lead.

We do need to know where to go to recharge our own spiritual batteries. It may be a variety of places for each person.

Where is God in this text? God is inviting us to grow closer to him by traveling the journey of faith with Jesus. This includes the reality of the cross experiences, as well as new life after every death. This is the good news of the gospel. Our faith is not in vain. Our Christ is real. Our faith has a strong base here — at Trinity Lutheran Church. We are committed to building that base of faith in our ministries in this interim time of ministry together. We need all the disciples we can get doing ministry of time, talents, money, and resources.

To conclude: in the 2008 movie Gran Torino (2008), Clint Eastwood played Walt Kowalski, a recently widowed racist retired Korean War veteran, and American auto worker who Highland Park Detroit, Michigan, neighborhood had changed. It had gone from working class families to various ethnic groups as neighbors. He scowled and was perpetually angry as he observed the decline in many neighborhood blocks. There was one Hmong family who lived next door him. One night he caught the Hmong boy named Thao trying to steal his 1972 vintage Gran Torino car.

The Hmong family was shamed by this act and made the boy work for Walt by doing yard work. The viewer learned that Walt's own adult children had long moved out to the suburbs and drove foreign made cars. They wanted to quickly send him off to a retirement community. Walt cussed them out. Walt continued to use various ethnic slurs throughout the movie, as he repaired family washing machines, light fixtures, and donated a deep freezer to them.

As the movie went on, Walt grew fond of the Hmong boy, Thao. He taught Thao about tools and various tips for building construction. Thao became an apprentice or disciple of Walt Kowalski. Walt got Thao a job, but saw the boy was still being harassed by gangs. After Thao's sister Sue was attacked, Walt decided if this boy was going to have any chance to make a decent living and grow up as an adult, he had to find a way to confront the gang. It led to his death.

Upon Walt's death, the young Catholic priest Father Janovich eulogized, "Walt Kowalski once said to me that I knew nothing about life or death, because I was an over-educated, 27-year-old virgin who held the hand of superstitious old women and promised them eternity. Walt definitely had no problem calling it like he saw it. But he was right. I knew really nothing about life or death, until I got to know Walt... and boy, did I learn."

As the movie ends, Thao Van Lor inherited the Gran Torino car that Walt's spoiled, suburban niece desired or coveted for herself. The boy Thao drove along the river shore with Walt's dog Daisey. Possibly Thao Van Lor had his transfiguration values moment while working with Walk Kowalski around the house and neighbor's house and yards.

Today, Transfiguration Sunday invites us to grow closer to Christ in our faith journey so that people can see our faith in our faces and actions. We will not have to announce anything to them. They will sense that we know who we are, and where our true confidence in life lays — in Jesus the crucified and risen Savior.

Amen.

Works Cited

- *DirecTV TCM [Accessed 04.15.2-23]*

- Fitzmyer, Joseph. *The Anchor Bible: The Gospel According to Luke, I-IX,* (Garden City, New York: Doubleday, 1981).

- Tiede, David. *Augsburg Commentary on The New Testament: Luke,* (Minneapolis, MN: Augsburg Fortress, 1988).

- Wilton, Carlos. *Lectionary Preaching Workbook: Series VIII, Cycle C.,* (Lima, OH: CSS Publishers, 2006).